Ann Carr's
Recipe
Collection

Illustrated by Martin MacKeown

MEREHURST PRESS
LONDON

NOTES ON THE RECIPES

1. Unless specific details are given in the individual recipes, the following apply:
- all recipes serve 6 people
- spoon measurements are level
- sugar is granulated
- eggs are standard size

2. Follow either the imperial measurements or the metric but do not mix them, as they have been calculated separately.

3. As individual oven temperatures vary, use the timings in the recipes as a guide. Always preheat your oven or grill.

The Publishers wish to thank Rosemary Wilkinson and Malcolm Saunders for their help with this book.

Published 1987 by Merehurst Press
5 Great James Street
London WC1N 3DA

Produced by Malcolm Saunders Publishing Ltd
26 Ornan Road
London NW3 4QB

CONVERSION CHART

US terms are given in brackets in the ingredients lists. Wax paper should be used where greaseproof is stated in the method. Here are some standard conversions for cup measurements:

	Imperial (Metric)	American
	2 fl oz (60 ml)	scant $\frac{1}{3}$ cup
	4 tablespoons	$\frac{1}{4}$ cup
	6 tablespoons	$\frac{1}{2}$ cup
	5 fl oz (155 ml)	$\frac{2}{3}$ cup
	6 fl oz (185 ml)	$\frac{3}{4}$ cup
	8 fl oz (250 ml)	1 cup
butter	8 oz (250 g)	1 cup
cheese, grated	4 oz (125 g)	1 cup
cream	5 fl oz (155ml)	$\frac{1}{2}$ cup
dried fruit	5-6 oz (155-185g)	1 cup
flour	4 oz (125g)	1 cup
nuts, chopped	4 oz (125g)	1 cup
rice, uncooked	7 oz (220g)	1 cup
sugar, granulated or caster (superfine)	8 oz (250g)	1 cup
sugar, brown	6 oz (185g)	1 cup
sugar, icing (powdered)	4-5 oz (125-155g)	1 cup

Copyright © 1987 this edition Malcolm Saunders Publishing Ltd
Copyright © 1987 text Ann Carr
Copyright © 1987 design, illustrations and hand-lettering Martin MacKeown

ISBN 0 948075 73 2

Reproduction by RCS Graphics Ltd.
Printed in Spain by Sirven Grafic, Barcelona

Contents

Introduction

SINCE CHILDHOOD I have collected recipes. For years they have lain in a kitchen drawer, held together with paperclips and clothes pegs. It wasn't until I finally stopped running restaurants that I actually had time to open the drawer and sort through the dog-eared papers and yellowing cuttings.

As I sorted through my collection I realised that each recipe related to a particular area of my kitchen and cooking. There were recipes for foods that needed long, slow cooking – the range section. For dry goods on the kitchen shelf I found recipes for Rice Cake, for family favourites, and for preserves for the larder. There were recipes for spices from the spice cupboard; for day-to-day ingredients from the fridge; for fresh foods for long storage in the freezer as well as seasonal recipes for spring, summer, autumn and winter. And a very fat clip of recipes for festivals, birthdays and Christmas.

As I browsed through these stained notes and cuttings I realised that they were not only a collection of recipes but a reminder that I have lived and worked in many kitchens, in many climates and in many countries. All have influenced me. Not only have I cooked for years in restaurant kitchens full of labour-saving equipment, but I have also cooked in some very primitive kitchens. One I particularly remember was in a remote village in south-west Turkey — another in a studio-flat in Chelsea. In London the water came out of a tap as did the gas for the cooker, and nearby were shops full of ingredients. In Turkey, in another world, the fire was made from gathered wood on an open hearth, the water was drawn in buckets from a well and the ingredients came from the fields.

My grandmother's kitchen in Ireland was very different: a large room in pale cream and green with fly papers hanging from the ceiling and the walls hung with great silver meat covers. Outside, a yard was filled with what seemed to me a

mountain of coke to feed the stoves. Off this kitchen were sculleries, larders, pantries and a wash-house. I was allowed into this paradise only occasionally: for the kitchen and Mary, the cook, were sealed off from the house by a green baize door.

While I was at school a friend introduced me to my first foreign kitchen. Her German mother's store-cupboards were full of strange things with unfamiliar smells and on the floor stood a crock of sauerkraut. Meals in that house were very special: red cabbage cooked with apples — I still use that recipe, given to me when I was a child — pork with red wine, hard spicy biscuits. All so different from what I was accustomed to.

On leaving school I went to Paris; not, ostensibly, to learn to cook, but to learn French. I learned to cook! Madame considered the English attitude to food rather lacking in finesse, and thought that that of the Irish must be absolutely barbaric, so she handed me over to her Normandy cook to see what could be done.

My first lesson in making mayonnaise took place in another kitchen in Paris; one which truly shocked me. It was a long, dark, windowless corridor. The walls were hung with pots and pans and sieves and all sorts of kitchen things. There was a stone sink and a stove that hissed and popped to cook the vegetables. From this hot, dark hole came the most wonderful and delicious meals. How well I remember the garlic, olive oil, wine, long baguettes, 'filet au poivre' and my first 'al dente' vegetables.

It was from kitchens such as that terrible black corridor in the centre of Paris, where fridges would have been luxuries and microwave ovens undreamt of and where the purées were made by laboriously sieving fruit or vegetables — no food processors then! — that wonderful and exquisite dishes were produced. It was in just such kitchens that my first serious cookery lessons took place and that many of the notes were made on which the recipes in this book are based.

Ann Carr

ACKNOWLEDGEMENTS

I owe special thanks to Rosemary Wilkinson, my editor, and also to Malcolm Saunders for their constant help and perseverance in putting this book together. And to Robin Woodhouse for his generous and expert assistance on wine. I would also like to thank many members of my family and many friends (some of them restaurant customers of mine) for their tasting and testing of these recipes. And, above all, I thank my husband, not only for his tasks of hand-lettering and illustration, but also for his endless endurance in eating experimental dishes.

The Kitchen Shelf

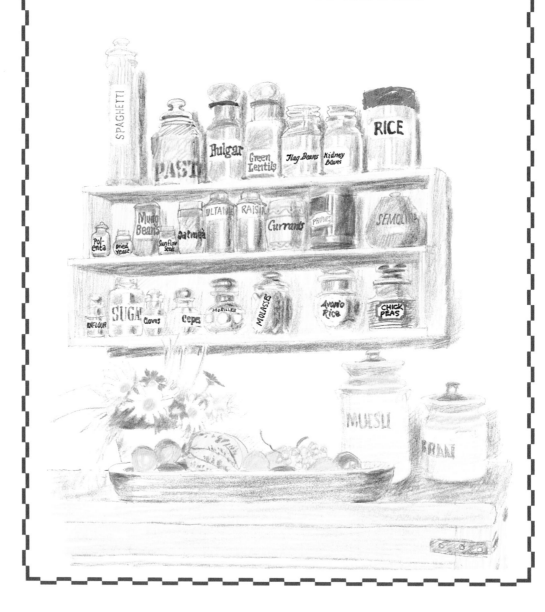

IN THE nineteenth century a well-stocked kitchen was not only a sign of more prosperous times, it was also essential for the continuation of good eating throughout the year. Now in the late twentieth century we live in a world in which it is possible to do without any storage at home at all. I well remember being aghast at a friend's once well-stocked but now empty shelves. When I asked her about their desolation she told me that the supermarket was now her kitchen shelf. Of course it is possible to live like that. It can be argued that it is cheaper: nothing ever goes off as it waits for an emergency that does not arise in time.

But isn't it more fun for the creative cook to have lots of ingredients stored on the shelves ready to be selected for favourite recipes or used to adapt them for the arrival of unexpected guests?

The ingredients which you keep on your kitchen shelf are, together with your own ingenuity, the basis of what you will cook.

To write a list of what one needs, apart from the obvious basics, such as tea, coffee, flour, salt, sugar, a few dried herbs and spices, is for me impossible, for my mind wanders off to the most exotic markets and exclusive shops and my list would include luxuries from many countries. Probably these

expensive ingredients would sit on my shelf till they were old and fusty – too precious to use – when my family would complain of waste. So my shelf is actually full of common place ingredients that I know I shall use and have many times turned to and been glad to find that the jars are full and the packets not quite empty.

Once I even stuffed a chicken with muesli – there seemed nothing else suitable and quick and there certainly wasn't enough bread to spare – and it was amazingly good. I think I took a couple of handfuls of muesli, chopped an onion and cooked it gently in butter or cooking oil, added an egg, salt, pepper and some spice – mace or ginger – stuffed the chicken, covered it with buttered paper and roasted it. Stuffed in this manner and stretched further with sausages roasted round its sides, it fed the family and the unexpected guest.

On my kitchen shelf I also keep some good, basic recipe books. I still use one that was school issue, old, battered and grease-stained, but ever useful. Someone once came to our kitchen and, after casting a critical eye at my modest collection on the shelf, remarked "I never use cookery books: the best food is inspired." All very well, but where is the inspiration to come from without the cookery book? Few people have grandmother's old 'receipt book' and the tradition of passing on an unwritten recipe by example died when the first convenience foods reached the markets. At that point, instead of mother teaching her children to take a large handful of this and a small handful of that to make a meal, a can of instantly consumable food could be bought, opened, heated and eaten. Now more than ever the cookery book has a place on the kitchen shelf.

I have specially valued ethnic cookery books for, without these, how could I make pasta and rice dishes from Italy, mild and delicate curries from India and Chinese meals far removed from those that the local 'takeaway' sells?

Amongst my collection I have some old, old books ~ nothing of great value ~ but books full of strange recipes and concoctions: tansy being one example. I had always thought of tansy just as a fruit custard, but it can also be a mixture of the juice of boiled spinach leaves and the herb tansy, strained and bottled, giving a strong, dark green concentrate used for flavouring and colouring.

My grandmothers and great aunts left notebooks full of the recipes of the period, the recipes often given family names, such as the puddings 'Snuff Box' or 'Strangford Mud'. We have carried on that tradition and a favourite family recipe has the undignified name 'Semolina Mush'.

Semolina Mush

Semolina has stood me in good stead and for years has made healthy suppers for hungry teenagers. My ingredients are measured in spoonfuls and cupfuls, since it is after all a pot luck meal and one adds or subtracts according to the appetites and numbers who arrive, unexpected or hungry.

2 tablespoons butter
1 cup milk
salt and pepper, to taste
2 rounded tablespoons semolina
4 eggs
1 cup grated cheese ~ a mixture will do
grated nutmeg

Melt butter in a saucepan, pour in milk, add salt and pepper, sprinkle on semolina and stir constantly to avoid lumps. Cook gently over a slow heat until mixture thickens, stirring all the time. When mixture is thick, remove from heat and beat in eggs one by one. The more you beat now the lighter the semolina will be. Add cheese and pour into a well-buttered ovenproof dish. Dust with grated nutmeg and bake at 220°C (425°F/Gas 7) for 30-35 minutes. The top will be brown and crisp.

You could use polenta ~ a grainy-textured corn meal ~ to make this dish. And sweetcorn kernels would give texture if you added half a cupful to the polenta and milk mixture. Serve with a mixed salad.

Rice is a splendid standby on the kitchen shelf and can quickly be turned into any number of nourishing dishes by adding cheese, tomatoes, left-over cold meat or fish. Bulgar ~ cracked wheat ~ may not be so well-known but is, perhaps, even more versatile than rice. It is cooked in the same way. Most dried beans and peas need long soaking and slow cooking, so they aren't much good for instant meals.

But the other of the three pulses, lentils, can be turned into the basis of a wholesome meal reasonably quickly, since most lentils nowadays seem to require only a short soak and are quick to cook. Flour is, of course, the obvious standby for with flour and water alone something edible can be made (however unpalatable). But with a few more ingredients you could make this:

Date & Walnut Loaf

6 oz (185g) chopped dates
6 fl oz (185ml) hot milk
2 oz (60g) butter or margarine
1 teaspoon ground cloves
¼ teaspoon grated nutmeg
1 teaspoon baking powder
2 oz (60g) bran
6 oz (185g) self-raising flour
3 oz (90g) brown sugar
2 oz (60g) chopped walnuts
1 egg, beaten

Grease a 2 lb (1kg) loaf tin. Place dates in a small bowl and pour over milk.

Melt butter or margarine and stir in, then allow to cool. In another bowl add spices, bran and baking powder to flour and mix well together. Stir in sugar and walnuts, then pour in milk and date mixture. Add beaten egg and mix well, adding a little water if the mixture seems too stiff. Pour into prepared loaf tin and bake at 190°C (375°F/Gas 5) until firm in middle, approx. 40 minutes. Leave for 5 minutes, then turn out on a wire rack to cool. Serve sliced and buttered.

Tuna Fish Pâté

Tuna fish is a useful standby for quick meals, such as this starter using canned stores from my shelf. It is a very filling pâté. Served with a tomato salad it makes a light meal.

7 oz (220g) can tuna fish
4 oz (125g) curd cheese
2 tablespoons tomato purée
2 cloves garlic, crushed
2 tablespoons vinaigrette
2 tablespoons milk
lots of freshly ground black pepper

Place all the ingredients in a bowl and beat well together until very smooth, or process in a blender. Pile into a serving dish and chill well. Serve with hot toast. A dish of black olives is a good garnish.

Pease Pudding Soup

Pease pudding can be bought canned. It comes out of the can almost solid and is very nourishing.

2 tablespoons butter
½ onion, finely chopped
pinch of mace
two 15 oz (470g) cans pease pudding
20 fl oz (625 ml) milk
30 fl oz (940 ml) meat or vegetable stock
6 fl oz (185 ml) cream, if desired

Melt butter in a saucepan, add onion and gently cook until tender and transparent, do not brown. Add mace. Mix pease pudding with milk, then add to pan, pour in stock and mix well together. Heat and serve. A swirl of cream is good on top.

Red Lentil Soup

2 oz (60g) butter

1 onion, finely chopped

1 clove garlic, crushed

4 carrots, diced

8 oz (250g) red lentils

½ teaspoon cinnamon

20 fl oz (625 ml) stock or bouillon

14 oz (440g) can tomatoes, chopped
   with juice

1 tablespoon chopped fresh basil or
   1 teaspoon dried

salt and pepper, to taste

4 fl oz (125 ml) cream or creamy milk,
   to finish

Melt butter in a large, heavy-bottomed saucepan, add onion and garlic and fry until soft but not coloured. When tender, add carrots and cook for 5 minutes, stirring continuously. Stir in lentils and cinnamon, then pour on stock, tomatoes and their juice. If using dried basil, add to stock. Cover and simmer until lentils are cooked and mushy, 1-1½ hours. Add fresh basil, salt and pepper, then cream or milk.

Lentils with Yogurt

An adaptation of a lentil dish I first tasted in a friend's kitchen in South-west Turkey.

THE LENTILS

8 oz (250g) lentils - large green
   preferred

1 onion

4 cardamon pods, whole

1 orange stuck with 2 cloves

salt, to taste

THE YOGURT

2 tablespoons olive oil

½ onion, finely chopped

2 cloves garlic, chopped

1 teaspoon ground cumin

1 teaspoon ground coriander

6 fl oz (185 ml) plain yogurt

Soak lentils in cold water for 2 hours, drain, rinse, then place in a large saucepan in plenty of water with onion, cardamon pods and orange stuck with cloves. Bring to the boil and simmer for 2 hours, adding salt just before cooking is finished. Drain, discard onion, cardamon and orange and keep warm.

In a small frying pan put olive oil (for this recipe olive oil is best), onion and garlic. Cook gently, taking care not to brown. When pale and tender stir in cumin and coriander.

To serve, place lentils in a warm, ovenproof dish. Pour over yogurt ~ use more yogurt than specified if you like, then pour the onion, oil and spice mixture over the yogurt.

Flageolet Beans with Dill

I keep a selection of dried beans ~ these are a favourite.

1 lb (500g) flageolet beans
salt and pepper, to taste
2 oz (60g) butter
2 onions, finely chopped
4 oz (125g) cream or curd cheese (or half and half)
6 fl oz (185 ml) plain yogurt
bunch chopped fresh dill

Soak beans overnight. Drain, rinse and place in a large saucepan with plenty of boiling water. Bring back to the boil and simmer for ¾ –1 hour until tender, adding salt just before cooking is finished. Drain and keep warm. Melt butter in a small saucepan, add onion and fry until soft but not browned. Add cream or cheese and pepper to pan, pour in yogurt and mix thoroughly. Reheat gently, do not boil. Add dill and pour mixture over beans.

Flageolet Bean Purée

Recently we ate in a restaurant where the first spring lamb was accompanied by a delicious purée of flageolet beans flavoured with garlic, butter and cream. So, if lamb is in season before mint, flageolet beans make the perfect alternative accompaniment.

8 oz (250g) flageolet beans
1 clove garlic, crushed
6 fl oz (185 ml) cream
salt and pepper, to taste

Soak and cook beans as described in 'Flageolet Beans with Dill'. Drain and purée in a blender or food processor. Add garlic, cream, salt and pepper and purée again. Reheat in a small saucepan and serve to accompany roast lamb.

Red Kidney Beans & Tuna Fish Salad

As well as dried beans on my kitchen shelf I keep a few canned beans. This salad makes a quick summer lunch or supper dish. It is best made half an hour before serving.

To serve 4 people you will need:

15 oz (470g) can red kidney beans
7 oz (220g) can tuna fish, flaked
4 spring onions (scallions), chopped
3 in (7.5 cm) piece of cucumber, cubed
4 firm ripe tomatoes, cut in wedges
2 hard-boiled eggs, peeled and sliced
6 tablespoons vinaigrette
chopped fresh parsley or coriander, if available

Place all the ingredients in a salad bowl and toss gently. Fresh bread and a green salad are all you need to accompany this dish.

Haricot Bean Pot

A one pot meal which makes a good supper dish.

1 lb (500g) haricot beans
2 onions
2 bay leaves
salt and pepper, to taste
2 tablespoons oil
14 oz (440g) can tomatoes, chopped with juice
small bunch fresh basil (or parsley), chopped
1 bunch spring onions (scallions), chopped
1 tablespoon butter, if desired

Soak beans overnight. Drain, rinse and put in a saucepan with one of the onions, left whole, and bay leaves. Bring to the boil and simmer until tender, 1-1½ hours, adding salt just before cooking is finished. Drain, discard bay leaves and set aside. Chop the remaining onion, put in a small saucepan with the oil and cook gently until soft but not browned. Add tomatoes, increase heat and cook until reduced by half. Add salt and pepper as well as basil or parsley, spring onions and butter, if desired. Pour over beans, gently reheat and serve. Chopped bacon or ham may be added, or hard-boiled eggs, but the Haricot Bean Pot is best served with a crisp green salad in summer or coleslaw in winter.

Pasta

The Italian influence on our eating habits is strong: pizza and spaghetti are now well-entrenched in the national diet. Dried pasta makes a quick and sustaining dish for the unexpected guest. It is easy to store, quick to cook and requires no advance preparation in a simple recipe such as this.

Take 8oz (250g) pasta, strew it into a large saucepan of boiling water. Boil for 7-9 minutes. Try to keep it <u>al dente</u>, that is firm to touch, not flabby (which,

by the time it's eaten, means soggy). Drain. In a pan large enough to hold all the cooked pasta easily with room to turn over, place 2 tablespoons grated Parmesan and stir in 6 fl oz (185ml) cream. Add a nut of butter, salt and freshly ground pepper. Add pasta, toss well and carefully. Serve at once.

Chopped fresh basil is very good with this, or chives, added to the cream and cheese mixture. We serve this dish accompanied only by a tomato salad, but it's good too with a roasted or grilled meat dish.

Home-Made Pasta Verde

Easy to make even if you haven't a pasta machine.

1 lb (500g) plain (all-purpose) flour
4 small or 3 large eggs
3 oz (90g) cooked spinach, squeezed very dry
2 teaspoons olive oil

Traditionally the flour is sifted onto a baking board but a wide, shallow bowl will do and is easier. Make a well in the centre of the flour, break eggs one by one into a cup and add to flour. Add spinach and oil. Draw flour up over eggs and spinach and, using fingertips, work all together. The dough will be fairly stiff to start with but as you work it will become more pliable. Knead thoroughly for 10 minutes. Cover with a damp cloth and leave

to rest in a cool place for 30 minutes.
    Break dough into pieces of a manageable size for your work surface and rolling pin: your noodles needn't be extra long, 12 in (30cm) will do. Lightly flour the surface and roll out dough very thinly. Take a sharp knife and cut into narrow strips, approx. ¼ in (0.5cm) wide. These strips can be gently folded into 'nests' and left on a clean teatowel in a cool place until you need them, or they can be hung over the back of a kitchen chair, first covered with a clean teatowel, or a clothes-horse will do (lock pets out).
    For plain egg pasta use 6 small or 5 large eggs and leave out the spinach.

Rice

Years ago when we were struggling hard and the children were small, we decided to go out for an Italian meal to celebrate the sale of some of my husband's work. Italian food was, we innocently thought, affordable. But even from the outside the restaurant we'd chosen looked rather too expensive. However, we had chosen this particular restaurant and eat in it we would. Once inside and settled at our table with damask cloth and crisp white napkins, the menu trembling in our hands, we realised that all we could possibly afford to eat would be one course. We looked again and found that if we were to enjoy wine with our meal it would not only be one course but one item. My husband summoned the waiter and bravely ordered Risotto alla Milanese ~ yes for two ~ and a bottle of red wine.

How well I remember that meal and the taste of that simply wonderful, pale yellow risotto! Often now as we serve rice to accompany a dish I think "why don't people just eat simple risotto, by itself, as we once did?"

Risotto alla Milanese

For the best results this classic recipe needs a well-flavoured, meat-based stock, e.g. veal or chicken. A stock (bouillon) cube can of course be used; so too can a pure vegetable stock, but it won't make a true risotto alla milanese. (There is no salt as it is assumed the stock is already salted.)

4 oz (125g) butter
1 small onion, finely chopped
1 marrow bone, from which you
    need 1 oz (30g) marrow
10 fl oz (315 ml) dry white wine
1 lb (500g) long-grain Italian rice
40 fl oz (1.25 litres) boiling meat stock
pinch saffron
3 oz (90g) grated Parmesan, plus
    extra to serve

Melt half the butter in a large heavy pan and gently fry onion and bone marrow until transparent. Add wine, increase heat and cook until reduced by about a quarter. Stir in rice and fry gently, stirring well to make sure it all gets well coated with wine mixture. Pour over half the stock, stir again, add saffron, then cover with a tight-fitting lid and simmer. As liquid gets absorbed add the remaining hot stock, stir, cover and continue to cook, stirring often and taking care risotto does not burn, for 20-25 minutes. When cooked, add remaining butter and Parmesan. Stir, cover and leave to settle for 2-3 minutes. Serve at once and offer a bowl of freshly grated Parmesan.

Prunes are magical with some meat dishes and it is well known that prunes and bacon complement each other: the savoury "Devils-on-Horseback" is famous. But don't just wrap up the stoned prune in bacon: add a bay leaf.

Bacon Rolls & Sweetcorn

For every slice of bacon (lean streaky is best) you will need:

1 bay leaf
1 prune, stoned
1 tablespoon cooking oil

SWEETCORN
two 11 oz (345 g) cans sweetcorn, drained
 and cooked
1 teaspoon grated lemon peel
knob of butter
pinch of mace or nutmeg
6 fl oz (185 ml) double (heavy) cream
salt and pepper, to taste

Remove rind from bacon. Roll up prune and bay leaf in bacon slice. Heat oil in a frying pan. Add bacon rolls, seam-side down, and fry gently for 10 minutes, turning frequently to ensure even cooking. They can also be grilled. Pull out bay leaf and discard before serving.

Put all the sweetcorn ingredients in a saucepan, stir well and heat thoroughly over a medium heat. Serve with the bacon rolls.

Rabbit with Bacon & Prunes

This is a dish we first ate in France.

2 oz (60g) butter
3½ - 4 lb (1.75-2 kg) rabbit, jointed
1 onion, chopped
4 oz (125g) streaky bacon slices, rinds
   removed and chopped
14 large prunes
2 bay leaves
6 fl oz (185 ml) dry white wine
4 teaspoons Dijon mustard
salt and pepper, to taste
6 fl oz (185 ml) cream

Melt half the butter in a deep, heavy-bottomed saucepan and add rabbit pieces. Brown all over, then remove. Add remaining butter and onion to pan and fry for 2 minutes stirring constantly. Add bacon, prunes and bay leaves. Return rabbit to pan and stir in wine and mustard. Cover tightly and cook very gently for 45 minutes. Taste for seasoning and add salt and pepper as necessary. Simmer for a further 15 minutes, until tender. Add cream and serve with plain, boiled potatoes.

Purée of Prunes with Chocolate

Chocolate and prunes are a superbly delicious combination. This pudding is very rich, so only a little is needed. The mixture could also be used to make a lovely pie filling. Canned prune purée is now available and could be used as a shortcut.

1 lb (500g) large prunes
thinly-pared peel of 1 orange
2 cloves
blade mace
2 oz (60g) sugar, if desired
2 oz (60g) butter
8 oz (250g) best quality plain (dark)
   chocolate

Most prunes nowadays are sold 'pre-soaked' but if yours are not you should of course soak them overnight, then drain. Place prunes in a sauce-pan with water to cover. Add orange peel, cloves, mace and sugar, if desired, and bring to the boil. Simmer for 10 minutes until tender. Cool, stone the prunes and purée in a blender or food processor. (You probably will not need the juice.) Return prune purée to pan and reheat, do not boil. Add butter and chocolate, remove pan from the heat and let butter and chocolate melt gradually. Mix well and pour into a serving dish, little ramekins or chocolate pots. Serve cold.

You may like to add some flavouring, try 2 tablespoons of rum.

Börek Stuffed with Spinach & Cottage Cheese

This is a recipe using basic ingredients from a Turkish kitchen shelf. It was prepared for me in early spring using edible weeds from the mountains and cheese made four months previously, salted and stored for later use. It was called "Otlu Börek" – weed pastry or, more precisely, a very fine, thin pastry stuffed with wild herbs. The pastry was mixed in a big bowl and left to rest while the herb and cheese mixture was prepared, then a cloth was placed on the floor and the börek table – a portable baking board – was taken off its hook on the wall and set down on the cloth. Next an extraordinary, long, thin rolling pin that tapered almost imperceptibly at both ends was placed ready on the cloth.

Making börek (filo) pastry is an art that requires many years of practice but if you would like to try it – and can resist the temptation to buy a packet at a good grocer's – here is the recipe:

1½ lb (750g) plain (all-purpose) flour
1 teaspoon salt
5 fl oz (155 ml) water
3 tablespoons olive oil

FILLING

1 lb (500g) fresh spinach, washed and
    drained
4 fl oz (125 ml) olive oil
4 spring onions (scallions), chopped
salt and pepper, to taste
pinch fresh cumin
8 oz (250g) cottage cheese, weighed after
    draining

Sift flour and salt into a large bowl, make a well in the centre and gradually add water and oil. Knead thoroughly for 5–7 minutes. Place dough in a bowl and cover with a damp cloth, while preparing the filling.

Roll up spinach leaves into tight rolls and, using a sharp knife, shred thinly. Place in a bowl, add oil, spring onions, salt, pepper and cumin. Toss well, add cheese and mix again.

Now comes the difficult part. Sprinkle your surface with flour and dust off most of it. Take a piece of the dough and roll it into a ball about 2 in (5 cm) in diameter. With the palm of your hand press it down onto the board

into a thin circle. Lift it, rub a little more flour onto the board, replace the dough circle and roll quickly and lightly until you have a paper-thin circle roughly 18 in (50 cm) across. You should get 18–20 circles of very thin pastry from the dough mixture. Reserve each by wrapping it with a damp cloth. Use as quickly as you can. Turkish village women fill and roll their sheets of pastry as they make them, so that they cannot dry out.

To finish, portion out the filling to match the number of pastry circles. Take one portion and sprinkle a little of it in a straight line near the edge of your first circle of pastry, roll over and sprinkle another line of filling, roll over and repeat until the portion of filling is used up and the circle all rolled. Pour ¼ in (0.5 cm) oil into a flan dish or sponge cake tin. Pack the completed rolls into dish or tin, spiral fashion, starting at the edge and working inwards towards the centre. Brush well with oil and bake in a hot oven, 230°C (450°F/ Gas 8), for 15–20 minutes until pale golden. The pastry should be crisp.

Bought filo pastry can be used in the same way, but remember to cover sheets not in use with a damp cloth.

Quick & Easy Brown Bread

This loaf needs only one rising and is very light and good.

2½ lb (1·25 kg) whole wheat flour
8 oz (250 g) strong white flour
½ oz (15 g) dried yeast or 1 oz (30 g) fresh (compressed) yeast
40 fl oz (1·25 litres) warm water
2 teaspoons salt

Grease three 1 lb (500 g) loaf tins or one 2 lb (1 kg) and one 1 lb (500 g) tin thoroughly. Mix the flours in a large bowl. Sprinkle or crumble yeast into water, add salt, stir and leave to dissolve and froth up. Pour over flour. Mix very thoroughly and pour into prepared loaf tins. Leave to rise in a warm place for about 45 minutes. Bake in a very hot oven, 230°C (450°F/Gas 8), for approximately 40 minutes. Turn out of tins at once and leave to cool on wire racks.

Butter Crumbs

This delicious topping is made by frying brown breadcrumbs in butter over a gentle heat, taking care not to burn. Add sugar and cinnamon to taste. The Butter Crumbs are best eaten warm sprinkled over stewed fruit. Apples are especially good and thick cream poured over makes it really scrummy. In Denmark a dessert of layered apple purée and breadcrumbs is called Veiled Lass.

A Savoury Biscuit (Cracker) Recipe

Tea and biscuits go together, so a tin of biscuits on the kitchen shelf is essential. 'Bath Oliver' biscuits are unsweetened but good with tea, coffee, wine, or cheese ~ or just by themselves if one feels peckish.

Dr William Oliver practised in the English spa city of Bath early in the eighteenth century. I like to think that his patients were much helped by the delicious biscuits he prescribed, for which the original recipe is said to be a closely-guarded secret. Bath Olivers are made commercially and bear the imprint of the great doctor's profile. Here is a homemade alternative to that famous savoury biscuit.

2 oz (60 g) butter
8 oz (250 g) strong white flour
good pinch salt
10 - 15 fl oz (315 - 470 ml) milk and
    water mixed

In a bowl rub butter into flour using fingertips, until well-mixed. Add salt to milk and water mixture, then gradually add to flour, to make a firm dough. The exact amount depends on the flour. Knead very well, roll out as thinly as possible and prick all over. Cut into rounds and place on a greased baking sheet. Bake in a very hot oven, 230°C (450°F/Gas 8), for 10-12 minutes. Do not allow to colour. They should be almost cream-coloured, never golden. Cool on a wire rack. Keep in an airtight container.

Sesame Seed Biscuits (Crackers)

4 oz (125g) plain (all-purpose) flour
freshly ground black pepper, to taste
pinch of cayenne pepper
3 oz (90g) butter or margarine
2 oz (60g) roasted sesame seeds
3 oz (90g) grated cheese
1 egg yolk

Sieve flour with peppers into a bowl. Rub in butter or margarine until mixture looks like fine breadcrumbs.

Add sesame seeds and cheese, then mix well together. Mix in egg yolk, press mixture together with the hands, divide into two and roll out fairly thinly on a floured board. Cut into rounds with a pastry cutter and bake in a moderately hot oven, 190°C (375°F / Gas 5), for 10-15 minutes. Leave for a few minutes before transferring to a wire rack to cool. Store in an airtight container.

Mayoress Cakes

Here is a recipe that uses just the kind of ingredients on any family kitchen shelf.

5 oz (155g) self-raising flour
3 oz (90g) desiccated coconut
2 oz (60g) crushed cornflakes
4 oz (125g) sugar
1 oz (30g) cocoa powder
6 oz (185g) butter or margarine, melted

CHOCOLATE ICING
2 oz (60g) butter or margarine
2 tablespoons milk
4 oz (125g) icing (powdered) sugar
2 oz (60g) cocoa powder
few drops vanilla essence

Mix together all the dry ingredients in a bowl. Pour over melted butter or margarine. Mix well, then press into a 12 x 8 in (30 x 20cm) Swiss roll (jelly roll) tin. Bake in a moderate oven, 160°C (325°F / Gas 3) for 30-35 minutes. Leave to cool in the tin.

Meanwhile, make the icing. Melt butter or margarine in the milk in a saucepan over a low heat. Remove from the heat and sieve in sugar and cocoa powder together. Add vanilla, beat well and pour over the cold cake mixture. Leave until cold, then cut into squares. Store in an airtight container. These keep well for up to two weeks.

Ginger Pancakes

These really are luxury pancakes. The mixture makes about eight 7 in (17.5cm) pancakes.

4 oz (125g) plain (all-purpose) flour
1 whole egg
1 egg yolk
3 tablespoons brandy
7-8 fl oz (220-250 ml) skimmed milk
1 teaspoon cinnamon
1 teaspoon grated fresh ginger
2 teaspoons icing (powdered) sugar

TO SERVE
freshly squeezed orange juice
caster sugar

Sieve flour into a bowl, make a well in the flour, add egg, egg yolk, brandy and milk and, with a wire whisk or electric beater, beat well until mixture is smooth and light. Leave to rest in a cold place for 30 minutes. The mixture can be left longer, any time up to 2 hours.

After the mixture has rested add cinnamon, ginger and sugar and beat well.

Next take a 7 in (17.5cm) heavy-bottomed frying pan and grease it with 3 tablespoons of best cooking oil. Pour off oil and with a ladle pour on some of your batter, tilt pan about until you have a very thin layer of batter covering bottom of pan. Cook for 1-1½ minutes over a medium-hot heat lifting edges with a palette knife to check that pancake is not burning ~ it should be cream and golden when it is cooked. When ready, turn with the help of palette knife and cook the other side. When both sides are ready, remove and place on a warm plate. Cover with slightly damp absorbent kitchen paper and keep warm in a very low oven. For each pancake proceed as above, pouring off oil between pancakes. This method ensures that your pancakes are not greasy and do not stick to your pan. It is a help to keep a special pan for pancakes. Serve the pancakes with orange juice and sugar.

Ginger Crunch

A lazy biscuit (cookie) recipe but very good indeed. Also quick to make.

8 oz (250g) butter
8 oz (250g) sugar
2 teaspoons ground ginger
14 oz (440g) self-raising flour

Melt butter and sugar gently in a saucepan. Remove from heat. Stir in ginger and flour and mix well together. Turn out into a 12x8 in (30x 20cm) Swiss roll (jelly roll) tin. Press well down. Bake in a moderately hot oven, 190°C (375°F/Gas 5) for 15-20 minutes until lightly browned. Cut into squares. Leave in tin until just warm. Transfer to a wire rack to cool.

Almond Frase

This is an 18th century recipe, half way between Helva and a fritter. It is rich but very delicious. Serve with raspberries or strawberries in summer or spiced peaches in winter.

6 oz (185g) ground almonds
2 oz (60g) cake crumbs or breadcrumbs
2 oz (60g) sugar
2 eggs, separated
2 egg yolks
6 fl oz (185 ml) single (light) cream
1 tablespoon rose water
½ oz (15g) butter

Mix together almonds, crumbs and sugar in a bowl. Beat the two egg whites together in another bowl until very stiff, and in a third bowl beat together the four egg yolks, cream and rose water. Pour egg yolk mixture over dry ingredients, mix well, then carefully fold in beaten egg whites.

Heat butter in a frying pan until it is frothy – do not let it burn. Drop spoonfuls of the mixture into hot butter and fry on both sides until golden brown. Serve hot.

Helva

Semolina Helva is very easy to make. Most recipes recommend that you make a sugar syrup with the sugar and water; this one is unusual in that the sugar is added dry to the semolina and the water slowly poured over. It is quick to make and delicious.

3 oz (90g) butter
6 oz (185g) semolina
8 oz (250g) sugar
1 teaspoon cinnamon
1 teaspoon mixed spice
2 oz (60g) chopped almonds
1 oz (30g) raisins

5 fl oz (155 ml) water
1 oz (30g) whole almonds

Melt butter in a heavy pan. Add semolina and fry, stirring and taking care not to burn, for approximately 3 minutes. Add sugar, spices, chopped nuts and raisins. Mix well. Stir in water, lower heat and cook for 10-15 minutes, stirring continuously. Pour into a heated serving dish and top with whole almonds.

A dish of thick cream is delicious with this Helva.

Rice Cake

This cake recipe comes from Italy. A caramel sauce is very good served with it.

bread, cake or biscuit crumbs
2 oz (60g) blanched almonds
40 fl oz (1·25 litres) milk
8 oz (250g) pudding (short grain) rice
6 oz (185g) sugar
4 eggs, separated
grated peel of 2 lemons
2 oz (60g) mixed citrus (candied) peel
1 tablespoon orange flower water
4-6 tablespoons rum

Butter an 8in (20cm) cake tin well and coat with crumbs. Toast almonds in a clean, dry frying pan over a low heat.

Leave to cool, then chop. Boil milk in a heavy pan, add rice and sugar and simmer gently until rice is just tender, about 30 minutes. Leave aside to cool. Beat egg yolks together and add to cooled rice mixture. Add lemon peel, mixed peel, chopped almonds and orange flower water. Whip egg whites until really stiff. Fold in to rice mixture. Pour into prepared tin and bake in a moderately hot oven, 190°C (375°F/Gas 5), for 1-1½ hours until firm to the touch and brown on top. Prick surface of cake with a needle or fork and pour over rum. Leave in the tin overnight. Turn out and cover with buttered crumbs. Serve in slices.

The Range

FIRE MAKES *heat: and satisfies a physical need. The most miserable* situation cheers up when the stove is lit and the kettle put on. Whether your kettle be electric or your stove gas or even microwave, the need for hot food will be fulfilled. One can still say, no matter how modern it is, that the stove is the heart and soul of the kitchen, just as the simple open hearth was long ago.

In the days of wood-burning stoves and ranges, a small team of helpers, hired or members of the family, was available to chop the wood for burning, to keep the kindling box full of dried sticks for hurrying along a slow fire and to stoke the stove during the day.

The type of fuel produced in an area - whether coal, reeds or wood, and, if wood, how old it was and how it had been cut - decided the type of stove used and therefore influenced the cooking.

A fine example of this was in Norfolk, England, where marsh reeds were used. These were tied in bundles: used upright they burned swiftly, giving out a quick, fierce heat for boiling pans on top of the stove or for searing roasts in the oven; used horizontally they smouldered slowly and the food could be simmered on top or baked very slowly in the oven. Many regions still produce specialities related to the limited cooking facilities of the past. In Norfolk you can still eat Norfolk

dumpling fast-boiled on top of the range or Norfolk Nobs, the recipe for which is given in this chapter, and which, as they originally were, are quickly baked in a hot oven, then left to dry in a slow one.

With the advent of coal, ranges and cookers changed. Coal was more versatile, stayed burning longer and could be slacked down for very slow burning. So the cooking range was redesigned to provide not only hot and cool plates on top but also an oven that was easier to regulate. A hot water boiler at the side was incorporated and a brass tap fitted to draw off the water. This was the forerunner of our modern boiler.

Gas and electricity brought yet another change to the range. The top cooking surfaces became hobs and the cooker was no longer a single, large unit producing wood ash or coal dust. The boiling hobs can now be on one side of the kitchen and a smart new eye-level oven on a wall opposite. With the introduction of microwave cookers both hob and oven can, at a pinch, be dispensed with, particularly in a confined living space, such as a bed-sitting room or a one-roomed flat.

No longer is a whole day's cooking done in order to make maximum use of the stove's temperature performance curve. At one time this meant making a pot-roast on the top and baking a whole series of foods, starting with bread when the oven was at its hottest and finishing with a slow-cooking dish, such as baked custard, as the stove was cooling.

There are still dishes that are best suited to your own cooking arrangements or your own working day.

Here is a lovely simple one-pot recipe using only one ring – gas or electric – or one hot plate on the modern version of the old range (and there are some excellent modern solid fuel ranges nowadays).

Pot Pie

Traditionally made with mutton but now with lamb as sheep are killed young. You will need a heavy, straight-sided saucepan with a tight-fitting lid for this dish.

Serves 4

2 lb (1 kg) stewing lamb, trimmed
    and cut into 1 in (2.5 cm) cubes
2 medium onions, finely chopped
2 carrots, sliced
2 sticks celery, chopped with leaves
10 fl oz (315 ml) stock or bouillon
salt and pepper, to taste
small bunch parsley, chopped.
8 oz (250 g) scone dough, see below

Layer meat, onions, carrots and celery in a saucepan, pour over stock, cover and simmer gently for 1½-2 hours or until meat is tender. Press out scone dough on a floured surface into a circle to fit the saucepan. Remove meat and vegetables from stove and season with salt and pepper, add parsley and cover carefully with the scone dough. Cover and simmer again for ½ - ¾ hour, until scone dough is well risen and cooked through.

SCONE DOUGH
8 oz (250 g) self-raising flour
salt and pepper, to taste
2 oz (60 g) butter or margarine or
    dripping
6 fl oz (185 ml) milk

In a bowl mix together flour, salt and pepper. Rub in fat with finger-tips until mixture resembles breadcrumbs. Add milk and mix quickly using a knife or a fork. The dough should be soft but not too wet.

Dried Pea Soup

Served with fried croûtons, this is a delicious one pot meal.

8 oz (250g) dried peas
2 tablespoons cooking oil
1 medium onion, finely chopped
2 carrots, diced
2 sticks celery, thinly sliced with
    leaves
8 oz (250g) streaky bacon or bacon
    trimmings, rinds removed and
    chopped
20 fl oz (625ml) meat or vegetable stock
20 fl oz (625ml) milk
salt and pepper, to taste

Soak dried peas in cold water overnight. Drain and rinse. Pour cooking oil into a saucepan, add onion, carrots and celery and cook for 2-3 minutes. Add bacon, cook for a further 2-3 minutes, then add peas and stock. Cover with a tight-fitting lid and simmer for 1-1½ hours, until peas are very soft and mushy, add milk and reheat. If during the cooking the soup looks too thick add some of the milk. Season with salt and pepper.

Pork Custard

An old-fashioned recipe which is a good way of using up cooked pork but it can also be made with fresh pork. This dish with its custard base would have been cooked after bread baking when the oven was cooling down, so that its custard base would not curdle.

1 lb (500g) cooked minced pork or fresh
    minced lean pork
4 oz (125g) fine breadcrumbs - brown
    or white
½ teaspoon ground cinnamon
¼ teaspoon ground mace
pinch of ground cloves
salt and pepper, to taste
1 teaspoon very finely chopped onion
    or 1 spring onion (scallion), chopped
4 eggs
20 fl oz (625ml) gravy or stock

In a bowl mix together pork, breadcrumbs, spices and salt and pepper. Add onion and mix lightly together. In another bowl beat eggs lightly, add gravy or stock and mix well. Butter a 2¼ pint (1.8 litre) pie or soufflé dish generously. Pour egg and gravy mixture over breadcrumbs and pork mixture. Gently and lightly mix together, then pour into pie dish. Stand pie dish in a tray of hot water and bake in a slow oven, 160°C (325°F / Gas 3), for 1½ hours. The custard should be set all through to the middle.

This is good served with baked potatoes and an Apple and Horseradish Sauce.

APPLE & HORSERADISH SAUCE
6 fl oz (185ml) apple purée – I like it
    slightly sweetened
3 teaspoons horseradish

2 tablespoons thick plain yogurt or
   sour cream

Beat the above ingredients together
and serve.

Hot Spiced Beef

A good winter dish using topside of beef and tenderising it with long, slow cooking.

2 tablespoons cooking oil
3-4 lb (1.5-2 kg) piece of topside,
   rolled and tied
10 pickling onions
6 medium carrots, left whole
2 cloves garlic
2 tablespoons brandy
2 tablespoons black treacle
2 medium cooking (tart) apples
1 sprig of fresh thyme or ½ teaspoon
   dried thyme
30 fl oz (940 ml) dry cider
20 allspice
4 bay leaves
salt and pepper, to taste

Heat oil in a large pan with a tight-fitting lid, add meat and brown all over. Add onions, carrots and garlic and fry gently until just browned. Add brandy and treacle. Cover tightly and leave to rest away from heat for 5-10 minutes while you peel and chop apples. Add apples, thyme, cider, allspice and bay leaves. Cover tightly again and simmer either on top of stove or in a moderate oven, 180°C (325°F/Gas 4), for 3½ hours. Half an hour before end of cooking time add salt and pepper. Discard bay leaves before serving.

Cabbage & Sausage Pot

A supper dish in which the sausages add flavouring to the cabbage.

1 large white cabbage
1 tablespoon cooking oil
1 medium onion, chopped
1 teaspoon brown sugar
1 teaspoon dill seeds, if desired
5 fl oz (155 ml) cider
1 lb (500 g) best pork sausages or a
    smoked pork boiling sausage
Salt and pepper, to taste

Trim cabbage of coarse outer leaves and tough stems, quarter and shred finely. In a heavy-bottomed pan with a tight-fitting lid, heat oil and add onion. Cook for 2-3 minutes, then add sugar, dill, if desired, and shredded cabbage. Mix well together, pour over cider and cover tightly. Cook very slowly for 30 minutes, remove from heat and add sausages. Cover and cook for a further $\frac{3}{4}$-1 hour, stirring occasionally to prevent burning. Ten minutes before end of cooking time add salt and pepper.

Pound Cake

Or in this case a half pound cake for I have halved the classic recipe, where the ingredients were given in one pound quantities.

8 oz (250 g) butter
8 oz (250 g) sugar
4 eggs
8 oz (250 g) self-raising flour
8 oz (250 g) currants
8 oz (250 g) sultanas

4 oz (125 g) mixed citrus (candied) peel
4 oz (125 g) glacé cherries
grated peel of one lemon
2 oz (60 g) finely chopped blanched
    almonds

Line an 8 in (20 cm) cake tin with greaseproof paper. Beat butter and sugar together in a bowl until light and fluffy. Add eggs one by one beating in between. Fold in flour gently, then add fruit, lemon peel and nuts. Turn into prepared tin and bake in a moderate oven, 160°C (325°F/Gas 3), for 3-3½ hours, until firm to the touch. Leave in tin for five minutes before turning out on a wire rack to cool.

Hasty Fruit Loaf

And tasty: this loaf freezes well, so make two.

8 oz (250 g) self-raising flour
4 oz (125 g) brown sugar
4 oz (125 g) currants
4 oz (125 g) raisins
4 oz (125 g) mixed citrus (candied) peel
grated peel and juice of one orange
2 oz (60 g) butter, melted
6 fl oz (185 ml) milk
1 egg, lightly beaten

Line a 2 lb (1 kg) loaf tin with buttered greaseproof paper. In a bowl mix together flour, sugar, currants, raisins, mixed peel and orange peel. Stir in butter, milk, beaten egg and orange juice and mix well together. Pour mixture into prepared tin and bake in a moderate oven, 180°C (350°F/Gas 4), for one hour, until firm to the touch. Leave in tin for five minutes before turning out on a wire rack to cool.

Three Grains Loaf

This bread freezes well so it is worth making a large amount at a time.

2 lb (1 kg) wholewheat flour
3 teaspoons salt
8 oz (250 g) bulgar
8 oz (250 g) medium oatmeal - oat flakes can be used
4 oz (125 g) sunflower seeds
1 tablespoon caraway seeds
1 oz (30 g) dried yeast or 2 oz (60 g) fresh (compressed) yeast
32 fl oz (1 litre) warm water

In a large bowl mix together flour, salt, bulgar and oatmeal. Add sunflower seeds and caraway seeds, mix again.

If using dried yeast, mix in a large jug with warm water. Leave in a warm place for 10 minutes until yeast is thoroughly dissolved. If using fresh yeast, cream in a small bowl with 2 tablespoons of the water; add rest of liquid and leave for five minutes. Make a well in flour mixture and pour in yeast and water. Mix all together and beat well either with a wooden spoon or in a mixer with a dough hook. Cover bowl with a clean cloth and leave to rise for ¾-1 hour or until dough has doubled in size. Meanwhile oil inside three 1 lb (500 g) loaf tins. With wooden spoon or dough

39

hook beat hard very thoroughly until dough is elastic. It is not necessary to knead this dough with the hands. Half-fill each tin with the bread mixture and leave again to rise for 30-45 minutes. Carefully place in a hot oven, 220°C (475°F/Gas 7) and bake for 50 minutes, until deep golden on top and bread begins to shrink from the side of the tin. Turn out onto wire racks to cool.

Norfolk Nobs

These would probably originally have been made with a sour dough starter rather than yeast as the raising agent.

1 lb (500g) plain (all-purpose) strong flour
1 teaspoon salt
4 fl oz (125 ml) milk or milk and water mixed
¼ oz (7g) dried yeast or ½ oz (15g) fresh (compressed) yeast
2 oz (60g) butter or margarine, melted
2 eggs, beaten

Sift flour and salt in a bowl. Warm milk and water to blood heat in a saucepan. If using dried yeast, sprinkle over the mixture and leave aside for 5-10 minutes, until yeast is dissolved. If using fresh yeast, cream in a small bowl with two tablespoons of the warm milk and water; add rest of liquid to warmed yeast and leave for 5 minutes. Make a well in flour and add melted butter, beaten eggs and yeast mixture. Work to a smooth dough and knead thoroughly. Cover bowl with a clean cloth and leave to rise until doubled in size, 30-45 minutes. Grease and flour a baking sheet.

Knock the dough down, roll out ¾ in (2 cm) thick and cut into 2 in (5cm) squares, place on prepared baking sheet and bake in a hot oven, 220°C (425°F/Gas 7), for 6-8 minutes. Remove from oven, reduce oven temperature to 120°C (250°F/Gas ½) and quickly split open bread nobs with a knife. Leave to dry out in oven for 1-2 hours. Cool on wire racks and store in an airtight container

The Larder

FLOUR

'PUTTING UP' preserves for the larder used to be an annual chore which began in early spring and carried on through summer into autumn: as each fruit or vegetable was picked at its prime and stored for future use during the long lean winter months. Before fridges and freezers became generally available, the stores on the larder shelves were essential to the survival of the family. What was not enjoyed fresh in its season was carefully conserved and the larder shelves were lined with jars of preserves, pickles, bottled fruits and potted meats. Crocks on the stone floor contained eggs in isinglass (a type of gelatine), fruit in alcohol, cider and home-brewed beers awaiting bottling. The hooks from the ceiling were hung with hams curing, sausages, dried fruits and vegetables, such as apple rings and mushrooms, onions and herbs in daily use and baskets of bread drying out of reach of rats and mice.

All this food in the larder meant that the housewife and her helpers had a very busy spring and summer, first picking, then sorting. Vegetables were dried, salted or pickled in brines and spiced vinegars. Dried herbs were distilled into medicinal brews for winter ills. Fruits were carefully picked and dried or turned into beautiful preserves in sugar and their own juices. Syrups and fruit vinegars were made as well as jams, jellies, fruit pastes and curds and fruit cheese. Meat was generally dealt with in the autumn, when the beasts were fat from lush summer grasses. With the colder weather the animals would have lost weight. The cooler days made it possible for the carcasses to be hung for a few days without getting fly-blown. They were then cut up and turned into hams, salt beef, dried beef, smoked mutton, cured pork, sausages, brawns, pâtés and potted meats.

Nowadays it is not essential to preserve and store for the family's survival. But a rich larder for one's family, friends and present-giving is still an intensely rewarding area of cooking. It enables one to avoid that frustrating aspect of feeding people: the knowledge that all one's hard work is scoffed at a single sitting! The larder-cook, on the contrary, can open the larder door and survey the results of the summer's labour. It is so satisfying to open, months later, a jar of spiced peaches to deck the Christmas ham.

It is relatively easy to buy jams and preserves labelled 'hand-made', but home-made is by far the better.

The huge walk-in larder of the past is no longer essential: a small airy cupboard in a cool place will suffice to store your hoard of goodies in.

Herb Powder for Winter Use

This is an old recipe for bouquet garni in powder form. Use it to flavour winter soups, stews and casseroles.

2 oz (60g) bunch of marjoram
2 oz (60g) bunch of winter savory
2 oz (60g) bunch of thyme
4 oz (125g) bunch parsley
grated peel of 4 lemons

Remove as much stalk as possible from herbs, tie in bundles and hang for 10-12 days in the airing cupboard or some other warm, dry place until brittle. Spread grated lemon peel out on greaseproof paper and dry with the herbs. When the herbs are ready, strip off leaves and pound all but tough stalks together with lemon peel in a pestle and mortar. Mix well with leaves and pack in small, air-tight containers.

Beef & Chestnut Casserole

This is an excellent party recipe which can be made as luxurious or kept as simple as you like depending on the optional additions of more chestnuts, cream and wine or brandy. Canned chestnuts in brine may be used but fresh are better.

3 lb (1.5 kg) stewing beef
3 medium onions, finely chopped or 8 oz (250g) button or pickling onions, left whole
8 oz (250g) celery stalks with their leaves, chopped
3 cloves garlic, chopped
4 tablespoons oil
12-16 oz (375-500g) peeled chestnuts
good bunch fresh marjoram (thyme or parsley can be substituted)
grated peel of ½ orange
10 fl oz (315 ml) red wine, if desired
20 fl oz (625 ml) stock or bouillon made from bouillon cubes
1 oz (30g) butter, if desired
1 oz (30g) flour, if desired
10 fl oz (315 ml) double (thick) cream, if desired
salt and freshly ground black or white pepper, to taste

Cut meat into roughly 1½ in (4 cm) cubes. In a heavy pan or casserole with a tight-fitting lid gently cook onions, celery and garlic in oil for 10 minutes, taking care not to brown. Add cubed meat and stir well, cooking gently for a further 5-10 minutes. Add chestnuts, herbs, peel and wine, cover tightly and cook for about 20 minutes, stirring occasionally to make sure the mixture doesn't stick and burn. Add stock or bouillon, replace lid and cook in oven, 160°C (320°F/Gas 3), or on top of stove slowly for 1-1½ hours. Fifteen minutes before end of cooking time add salt and pepper. Either serve straightaway or allow to cool, cover and keep for 1-2 days in larder or fridge. Heat through to serve.

FOOTNOTE Should you wish to thicken the gravy, mix the butter and flour to-gether in a small bowl, then stir the paste into the casserole. Cook for a few minutes until thickened. You can further enrich this sauce by adding the cream at this point. Do not boil again.

Mixed Fish Provençal

This recipe was originally given to me by a kind neighbour. I was an inexperienced cook and left out three of the ingredients at the proper stage, so that when I had the whole dish assembled I looked round my work area and there, to my horror, were the flour, butter and parsley that should have been incorporated – what was to be done?

In fact it was a very fortuitous mishap for I invented a topping that I think a vast improvement on the original dish, though the absence of the thick, glutinous sauce which the adding of the flour would have made perhaps removes the provençal influence. This dish is a great favourite with family and friends.

The recipe can be made more luxurious by the addition of more prawns, by using halibut instead of cod, or by adding crab or lobster instead of the full quantity of white fish.

My basic recipe is:

2 medium onions, finely chopped
4 cloves garlic, finely chopped
2 tablespoons olive oil
1 lb (500g) just ripe tomatoes, skinned and chopped or 14 oz (440g) can tomatoes, drained and chopped
2 tablespoons tomato purée

2 tablespoons chopped fresh parsley
salt and freshly ground black pepper, to taste
1½ lb (750g) cod, haddock or halibut, skinned
8 fl oz (250ml) white wine
2 tablespoons cornflour (cornstarch)
12 oz (375g) cooked peeled prawns

TOPPING
4 oz (125g) butter
8 oz (250g) plain (all-purpose) flour
4 tablespoons finely chopped fresh parsley

Put the onions, garlic and olive oil in a frying pan and cook gently until tender and well cooked. Do not brown. Add tomatoes and purée. Add 2 tablespoons of parsley, then salt and pepper; leave aside.

In a shallow pan gently poach fish in white wine, turning once. Five minutes per side is enough just to poach fish briefly as it only needs to be just cooked for it will be re-cooked in the oven. Remove fish, reserving stock, bone and flake keeping pieces as large as possible. Mix 2 tablespoons of fish stock with cornflour. Add to tomato and onion mixture. Add rest of stock and simmer until cornflour is cooked. Add fish and shellfish, salt and pepper. Pour into ovenproof dish.

To make the topping, either rub butter into flour in a bowl or blend in a food processor until mixture looks like fine breadcrumbs, add salt, pepper and parsley. Sprinkle over fish mixture. Bake for 15-20 minutes in a hot oven, 230°C (450°F/Gas 8) until topping is golden.

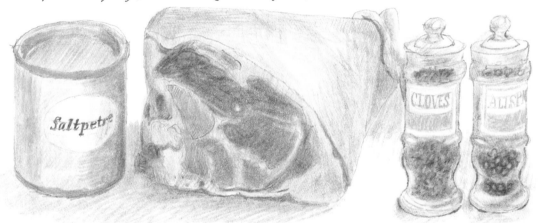

Mutton Hams

This is a very old recipe for curing a leg of mutton like ham. If you have a smoke box and access to mutton, this recipe is worth trying.

2 gallons (5 litres) cold water
2 lb (1 kg) salt
12 oz (375 g) brown sugar
1 oz (30 g) saltpetre
2 tablespoons allspice
12 cloves
leg of mutton weighing 5-6 lb (2.5-3 kg)

Put all the pickle ingredients in a large clean bucket. Place leg of mutton in pickle and keep it submerged with a lid and heavy weights. Keep in a cool place, check to ensure meat is well covered by brine and turn leg of mutton daily. On the fourth day, remove mutton from pickle, dry very thoroughly and hang in a smoke box. Smoke for 7-8 hours at 220-250°F/110-120°C. Delicious hot or cold.

45

Potted Beef or Tongue

This is a good way of using up a few miserable scraps from a family joint or the throat end of a tongue after the best part has been eaten hot. It's a good lunch or supper dish and keeps well if properly sealed with clarified butter.

8 oz (250 g) cooked meat
4 oz (125 g) butter, softened
2 tablespoons brandy, madeira or sherry,
    if desired
salt and pepper, to taste
pinch of mace
pinch of cayenne pepper
4 oz (125 g) clarified butter, see below

Chop meat into small pieces. Place meat and butter in a blender or food processor and process to a smooth paste, add brandy, madeira or sherry if desired, then salt, pepper and spices. Blend until well mixed, scraping down the sides of the bowl to ensure all ingredients are incorporated. Adjust seasonings if necessary. Spoon into small pots for keeping or one large pot for a family meal. Make sure the surface is level and cover completely with clarified butter. Keeps well in a cool place for about 1 week and up to 6 weeks in the fridge.

TO CLARIFY BUTTER

In a bowl over hot water or in a heavy-bottomed pan over a really low heat gently melt good fresh butter. Leave aside to rest for 10 minutes near heat. Skim if necessary and very slowly pour off the clear yellow butter, making sure that you leave all impurities at the bottom. I make at least 8 oz (250 g) of this at a time as it is useful for cooking with. Clarified butter burns at a much higher heat than unclarified and keeps for months covered in the refrigerator.

A Green Sauce

Another old recipe found with surprise in an old cookery book — with surprise because I had been making a sauce much like this for years and serving it with duck. It can also be served cold with meat left-overs.

8 oz (250 g) green gooseberries
1 handful of spinach leaves
6 fl oz (185 ml) dry white wine
½ oz (15 g) butter
1 oz (30 g) sugar

Top and tail gooseberries, wash spinach leaves and chop roughly. Place all five ingredients in a small saucepan with a tight-fitting lid and simmer gently until the gooseberries are very tender. Purée mixture in a blender or food processor, then reheat if necessary. To keep this sauce for 6-8 weeks, return purée to saucepan, bring to boil and boil gently for 2-3 minutes stirring constantly, then pot as for jam (see Dark Green Mint Jelly).

Pickled Mushrooms

Nowadays mushrooms are an all year round crop, so it may seem unnecessary to go to the bother of pickling them, but it is well worth pickling wild mushrooms not generally found in shops and markets. Makes approx. four 1 lb (500g) jars.

1 lb (500g) wild or very small cultivated mushrooms, wiped clean
20 floz (625 ml) white wine vinegar
18 black peppercorns
12 allspice, left whole
peel of 1 orange
small bunch marjoram
2 teaspoons sugar
½ teaspoon salt

Place vinegar, spices, orange peel, marjoram, sugar and salt in a saucepan and bring to the boil. Cover and leave to simmer for 20 minutes. Strain and return to the pan with mushrooms. Bring to boil, then simmer on a low heat for 10-15 minutes. Remove mushrooms with a slotted spoon and pack in clean, warm jars, top up with cooking liquor, seal tightly and store for 4 weeks before using. Will keep up to 1 year. Once opened, store in fridge.

Dark Green Mint Jelly

One of the pleasures of the larder that more than makes up for any hard labour put in on hot summer days is the joy of opening a jar of something delicious that tranforms a rather dull dish of left-overs, such as cold mutton.

3 lb (1.5 kg) cooking (tart) apples
1 lemon, sliced
40 floz (1.2 litres) water
1 lb (500g) sugar to every 20 floz (625ml) juice
a large bunch mint
2 teaspoons malt vinegar

Wipe and cut up apples, no need to peel or core. Place in a preserving pan or other large saucepan, add lemon, cover with water and simmer gently for ¾-1 hour, until fruit is soft and pulpy. Strain through a jelly bag, preferably overnight. Measure juice into preserving pan and to every 20 floz (625 ml) add 1 lb (500g) sugar.

Strip mint of leaves, add stalks to juice. Chop leaves and reserve. Bring slowly to boil until sugar is completely dissolved, then increase heat to a fast boil for 15-20 minutes, stirring gently until set. To test for set, remove pan from heat and put a little jelly on a cold plate, leave to cool. The jelly is setting if liquid begins to wrinkle when plate is tilted. If using a sugar thermometer 110°C or 220°F are the readings for setting jams and jellies. When 'set' is reached, remove from heat, add vinegar and chopped mint leaves. Return to heat and bring again to the boil. The jelly is now ready for potting.

To pot, jars should be clean, warm and dry. Remove any scum that may have formed and pot jelly carefully and quickly. Fill jars up to the brim, cover with wax circles, then seal with self-sealing lids or cellophane covers. Plastic wrap can be used. Label and store in a cool, dark cupboard or the larder.

Elderberry & Marjoram Jelly

Elderberries on their own have not enough pectin for quick setting, so apples are added to ensure a firm jelly. Marjoram complements the elderberry flavour and makes this a good jelly to accompany game or cold turkey at Christmas or Thanksgiving. This jelly is a lovely clear, ruby-red colour.

2 lb (1 kg) elderberries after stalks have been removed
20 fl oz (625 ml) water
2 lb (1 kg) cooking (tart) apples
1 lemon
1 lb (500 g) sugar per 20 fl oz (625 ml) juice
1 medium handful marjoram

Wash elderberries and strip from their stalks. Place in a pan with 10 fl oz (315 ml) water. Wipe and quarter apples – no need to peel or core. Place in another saucepan with the remaining water, the juice of the lemon and the cut-up lemon peel. Boil both fruits gently, covered with a tight-fitting lid. There is very little extra liquid so watch out for pan drying and fruit burning. When fruits are soft and pulpy, pour both fruits into a jelly bag and leave to drain overnight.

Measure juice into a preserving pan

and to each 20 fl oz (625 ml) of juice add 1 lb (500g) sugar. Add the marjoram bunch tied in a muslin bag. Slowly dissolve sugar, stirring gently. When sugar is dissolved, increase heat to a fast boil and boil until setting point is reached. (For setting point see Dark Green Mint Jelly). Remove herbs. Skim off any scum and pot in clean, warm jars, cover and store.

Rhubarb & Strawberry Jam

Rhubarb and strawberries seem to have an amazing affinity. In this jam the rhubarb balances the strawberries' over-sweetness without in any way impairing its wonderful flavour. In fact it seems to me to bring out and help retain a certain garden freshness in the fruit. I first tasted this jam in Switzerland and was doubtful if the combination could possibly work. However, I found it quite the best way of making a good strawberry jam. Do use only the best fruits available, don't pick slightly over-ripe or tired strawberries and don't use old rhubarb. Both will spoil the 'set' and therefore also the marvellous flavour.

4 lb (2 kg) strawberries, tops removed
2 lb (1 kg) rhubarb, trimmed, chopped
6 lb (3 kg) sugar
15 fl oz (470 ml) water

In two separate bowls soak prepared fruit with sugar, using 4 lb (2 kg) sugar for strawberries, 2 lb (1 kg) sugar for rhubarb. Stir occasionally and leave overnight. Next day pour both the rhubarb and strawberry mixtures into a preserving pan, add water and bring gently to the boil, taking care that all the sugar is dissolved before you boil the pan hard. Boil fast until 'set' is reached (see Dark Green Mint Jelly), 7-10 minutes. I like to have my strawberry jam slightly runny rather than to have the wonderful freshness of the fruit spoilt by over-boiling just to achieve a good 'set'!

For this jam allow the mixture to rest for 15-20 minutes before potting. This helps to prevent the fruit from rising to the top of jars. Remove scum and stir well to mix the fruit before potting in clean, warm jars. Cover and store.

Kumquats in White Wine

These small tart oranges the size of a pecan or walnut are well worth preserving. Use them to accompany duck as both a garnish and a relish, or slice them to fill a tart. They are good with gammon or boiled bacon or, sliced, improve a winter fruit salad.

Fill clean glass jars with 2 lb (1 kg) kumquats, pour over 40 fl oz (1.2 litres) boiling white wine. Seal jars tightly and keep 2-3 months before using. Once opened, store in fridge where, provided the fruit is covered by the wine, they will keep for another 2-3 months. Spices and sugar can be added to the wine but I like to leave the fruit unflavoured and use it to flavour other dishes.

Prunes in Rum

These make a delicious dessert served with whipped cream and lacy biscuits. Makes approx. four 1 lb (500 g) jars.

10 fl oz (315 ml) cold strong tea, strained
2 oz (60 g) brown sugar
thinly pared peel of one lemon
2 lb (1 kg) pitted prunes
10 fl oz (315 ml) dark rum

Mix together tea, sugar and lemon peel in a heavy-bottomed saucepan, boil hard, uncovered, for 5-8 minutes. Remove peel. Pack prunes into jars and half fill with hot syrup. Top up with rum, then seal tightly and store in cool, dark cupboard or larder. Allow flavour to mature for 3-4 weeks before opening. Will keep 2-3 months. Once opened, store in fridge.

If you cannot get pitted prunes, first poach prunes in covered saucepan in the cold tea for 10-15 minutes. Remove prunes with slotted spoon and stone carefully. Add sugar and lemon peel to juice and proceed as above.

50

Spiced Peaches

Makes approx. four 1 lb (500g) jars

2 fl oz (60 ml) white wine vinegar

2 lb (1 kg) peaches – small white peaches have more flavour than the large yellow variety

2 in (5 cm) cinnamon stick

4 whole cloves

6 allspice, left whole

4 oz (125g) brown sugar

10 fl oz (315 ml) water

thinly pared peel and juice of 1 orange

10 fl oz (315 ml) brandy

Measure vinegar into a shallow bowl big enough to hold the peaches when halved. Skin peaches, cut in half and remove stones. Toss at once in vinegar. Ripe peaches usually peel quite easily. Should some of your peaches be not quite ripe enough, plunge into boiling water, leave for 1½ minutes and peel. Drain and re-serve vinegar from peaches.

Combine spices, sugar, vinegar, water, orange juice and peel in a heavy sauce-pan, cover and boil for 5-8 minutes. Add peaches to spiced syrup a few at a time and poach gently. Remove with a slotted spoon.

Fill clean glass jars with peaches. Strain the syrup and pour over peaches to half-fill jars, then top up with brandy. Seal tightly. Store in a cool, dark cupboard or larder. Allow flavours to mature for 3-4 weeks before opening. Will keep 2-3 months. Once open, store in fridge.

Rich Chocolate Cake

This is a real larder cake for it definitely improves with keeping, and is at its best after 4-5 days on a cool larder shelf – in a cake-box of course! Fresh whipped cream flavoured with vanilla or a liqueur is the best filling and topping for this cake if you don't want to keep it once cut, but you can ice and fill it with this cream cheese icing, which will keep for 2-3 days. Very rich, but very good.

4 oz (125g) plain (dark) chocolate

4 oz (125g) butter

4 oz (125g) sugar

3 eggs, separated

3 oz (90g) ground almonds

4 oz (125g) stale cake crumbs

1 oz (30g) self-raising flour, sieved

ICING

6 oz (185g) cream cheese

1½ oz (45g) icing (powdered) sugar

1 teaspoon grated orange peel

1 oz (30g) finely chopped mixed peel

TO DECORATE

fresh orange segments

Break chocolate into pieces in a small bowl over hot water and leave to melt. Line two 8in (20cm) cake tins with non-stick paper. Cream butter and sugar together in a mixing bowl until light and fluffy. Add lightly beaten egg yolks a little at a time; beat well. Beat in chocolate which should not be too hot. Stir in almonds, cake crumbs and flour. Beat egg whites stiffly and carefully fold in.

Pour mixture into prepared cake tins and bake in a moderate oven, 180°C (350°F/Gas 4), for 20-25 minutes. The cakes are done when firm to touch and slightly shrunk from the sides of their tins.

Beat all the icing ingredients together in a bowl or process in a blender or food processor. Fill and ice the cake. Decorate with thin slices of fresh orange.

Betty's Lemon Cake

A Swiss cake, which keeps well for at least a week. Try not to eat for 2 days to allow the flavours to develop.

9 oz (280g) butter
9 oz (280g) sugar
grated peel and juice of 2 lemons
5 eggs
9 oz (280g) self-raising flour

ICING GLAZE
9 oz (280g) icing (powdered) sugar

Line a 2 lb (1kg) loaf tin with buttered greaseproof paper. In a bowl cream together butter and sugar until very light and fluffy. Stir in lemon peel. Add eggs one by one beating well between each. Fold in flour. Pour into prepared loaf tin and bake in a moderate oven, 200°C (400°F/Gas 6) for 40 minutes. Leave to cool in tin.

To make the icing, gently cook lemon juice and icing sugar together in a small saucepan until sugar dissolves. Do not allow to boil. When sugar is dissolved, stir well, then allow to cool slightly. Turn out cake when cooled, pour over icing and leave until set.

The Fridge
and the Freezer

THE FRIDGE is an extension of the larder, or indeed it _is_ the modern larder and, provided your food is carefully wrapped and manufacturers' instructions followed, you can store the food in your fridge from days to months.

Ideally the fridge is neatly packed with butter and eggs, bacon and meats well covered, jars of lemon curd and spiced peaches and bottles of home-made drinks. My fridge is not ideal. It is packed with such things as: a tired chicken carcass too good for the dog, but lacking enough meat for a family meal; one pickled mackerel which the cat won't eat; a cupful of cold pasta and vegetables from a previous supper. With luck there will be the usual butter,

eggs and cheese and, with more luck, a jar or two of vegetable stock, to help me utilise the left-overs.

I know I do not use my deep freeze to its utmost potential, but I do try to keep it stocked with some of the foods that I will use in my kitchen and also with some basic ingredients, such as tomato sauce, made from the summer's glut, as well as fish stock, which is so much easier to make ahead than when you are in the middle of a 'quenelle' recipe.

Fresh soft fruits are a joy to have, so too are the best of summer's vegetables. Fish must be very fresh for freezing, but the knuckle end of a leg of lamb is excellent, as are stewing steak, pie veal and venison.

Basic Vegetable Stock

You do not need to use your best, freshest vegetables for this very useful stock. Do add other clean, washed vegetables, peelings and even onion skins. Parsnips and cabbage leaves are best avoided, as they would over-flavour the stock.

60 fl oz (1·8 litres) water
4 carrots
2 onions
1 bunch parsley or parsley stalks
2 sticks celery, if desired
10 peppercorns
salt, to taste

Place all ingredients in a big pan, bring to the boil and simmer for 1½ hours. Drain, allow to cool and store, covered, in the fridge.

Pickled Mackerel

This is a recipe usually associated with herrings. Although mackerel is not as oily as herring this recipe suits the fish very well. Traditionally malt vinegar was used but wine vinegar is nicer and unless you want to keep the fish for several weeks or months, a mixture of wine vinegar and wine is even better. I like to use cider and cider vinegar. Should fennel fronds be unavailable, use one whole fennel bulb, sliced and layered with onion.

6 fat mackerel, gutted and cleaned
1 medium onion, thinly sliced
1 bunch fennel fronds
12 peppercorns
12 allspice
1 dried hot chilli
10 fl oz (315 ml) cider
10 fl oz (315 ml) cider vinegar
2 teaspoons sugar
1 teaspoon salt

Wash mackerel well in cold water. Lay half the onion and half the fennel on the bottom of a shallow dish (not aluminium), carefully arrange the mackerel on top and cover with the remaining onion and fennel. Sprinkle on pepper and spices. Mix cider, vinegar, sugar and salt together and pour over mackerel. Cover well with foil and bake at 180°C (350°F/Gas 4) for 40-50 minutes.

This dish is best eaten cold, plain new potatoes are good with it or a potato salad.

Pickled Mackerel Spread

2 oz (60 g) curd cheese
1 pickled cucumber, chopped
½ teaspoon finely chopped onion
finely ground black pepper, to taste
1 pickled mackerel, see above

In a bowl mix cheese, cucumber, onion and pepper together. Trim and bone mackerel (the bones will be soft) and beat into the curd cheese mixture. Use as a pâté or to fill sandwiches or picnic rolls. Keep covered in the fridge for 2-3 days.

Spiced Fish with Tomato

A marvellous starter: it only improves with keeping. Start one day ahead.

1½ lb (750g) cod fillets, skins removed
16 fl oz (500ml) water
4 bay leaves
4 slices lemon
8 fl oz (250ml) white wine vinegar
4 fl oz (125ml) olive oil
3 tablespoons tomato purée (paste)
1 teaspoon sugar
1 tablespoon paprika
¼ teaspoon chilli pepper
4 cloves garlic, crushed
2 onions, peeled and finely sliced
2 tablespoons fresh chopped parsley

Poach cod gently in water with bay leaves and lemon slices for 10 minutes or until just cooked. Remove using a slotted spoon and place in a shallow serving dish. Mix together vinegar, oil, tomato purée, sugar, spices and garlic and pour over fish, top with onion rings and leave to cool. When cold, cover with plastic wrap and place in the fridge. Leave overnight or longer. Sprinkle with chopped parsley just before serving.

Chicken Butter

This is a recipe for a cooked meat pâté to make use of a small amount of left-over chicken.

4 oz (125g) butter
grated peel and juice of 1 lemon
1 teaspoon chopped fresh thyme
1 cup cooked chicken, diced
salt and pepper, to taste
clarified butter, see page 46

In a blender or food processor blend butter until soft and creamy, then add lemon peel, juice and thyme. Blend well, add chicken and blend again until you have a fairly smooth paste. I like this paste a little coarse rather than too smooth. Season with salt and pepper, mixing well. Spoon into ramekins or small bowls and cover with a thin layer of clarified butter.

Pasta Fritters

Much better than they sound. Serve as a lunch snack with grilled tomatoes or bacon.

6 fl oz (185ml) milk
2 eggs
1 tablespoon self-raising flour
1 cup cooked pasta, roughly chopped
2 spring onions (scallions), chopped
salt and pepper, to taste
1-3 tablespoons cooking oil

Pour milk into a deep bowl, add eggs and beat well. Slowly sprinkle in flour, beating all the time. To this batter add pasta, spring onions, salt and pepper. Heat oil in a frying pan and drop the batter by spoonfuls into oil; fry on both sides until golden brown.

Cheese Left-Overs

Don't let little scraps of cheese dry out in fridge or larder. Grate them down and to every 8 oz (250g) add 2 oz (60g) butter and 2 tablespoons brandy, port or sherry, or just add a dash of Tabasco or Worcestershire sauce.

Beat together well, spoon into a pot and store covered. You can go on adding to this; it's useful for making quick cheese toast, adding to a sauce or vegetable topping or livening up mashed potatoes.

White Stock

Both this and the following fish stock are well worth making and freezing. You may not want to use them for general family cooking but it is extremely helpful to have a good stock available if a special recipe requires it.

2 lb (1 kg) knuckle of veal or chicken
    bones or both
2 onions
2 carrots
½ lemon
bunch of herbs, e.g. parsley, thyme,
    marjoram
100 fl oz (2.5 litres) water

Place bones, vegetables, lemon and herbs in a large saucepan and cover with water. Bring to the boil, cover and simmer for 3-4 hours, skim and strain. Leave overnight to get really cold, then skim again, removing any fat particles. Pour into containers and freeze.

Fish Stock

white fish trimmings and bones or a
    cod's head
1 onion
1 carrot
1 bay leaf
8 peppercorns
80 fl oz (2 litres) water

Wash the fish. Put in a saucepan with vegetables, bay leaf and peppercorns and cover with water. Bring to the boil, cover and simmer for 1½ hours. Strain, cool and pour into containers and freeze.

Ham & Parsley Mousse

A quick simple starter, light lunch or supper dish, using the remains of a cooked ham from the freezer.

1½ lb (750g) cooked lean ham, minced
4 tablespoons cider
½ oz (15g) gelatine
6 tablespoons fresh chopped parsley
6 fl oz (185 ml) double (heavy) cream,
    whipped
salt, to taste
plenty of freshly ground black pepper

Place minced ham in a bowl. Heat cider in a saucepan, sprinkle in gelatine and stir until dissolved. Remove from heat. Add parsley to ham, mix well, then fold in cream and add salt and pepper. Add cider and gelatine mixture, mixing well but gently. Pour into a soufflé dish and place in the fridge until set. Serve chilled with slices of hot brown toast and a tomato salad.

Lamb with Broad Beans

An excellent recipe for using frozen meat and vegetables.

3 tablespoons olive oil
2 medium onions, chopped
2 cloves garlic, chopped
2 knuckle ends of leg of lamb, whole
2 tablespoons chopped fresh dill
1 tablespoon vinegar
20 fl oz (625 ml) water
salt and pepper, to taste
1 teaspoon sugar
1 lb (500g) frozen broad beans
10 fl oz (315 ml) plain yogurt, to serve

Heat oil in a heavy saucepan with a tight-fitting lid, add onion and garlic and fry gently for 3-5 minutes. Trim lamb of fat, add to onion and garlic, turn over and over in the mixture for 5 minutes until well coated with oil, then add dill and vinegar and turn again. Pour over water, bring to the boil, cover tightly and simmer slowly for 1 hour. Remove lid and test for tenderness, add salt, pepper, sugar and broad beans. Cook for a further 15-20 minutes.

Just before serving pour over yogurt and gently heat, do not boil. I think this is best accompanied by a dish of plain boiled bulgar.

Casserole of Venison

2 oz (50g) butter or cooking oil
1 medium onion, chopped
2 lb (1 kg) venison, trimmed and cubed
1 large cooking (tart) apple
6 juniper berries
30 fl oz (940 ml) cider
salt and pepper, to taste
2 tablespoons brandy

Melt butter or oil in a saucepan with a tight-fitting lid, add onion and fry gently until soft but not coloured. Add venison and cook for 7-10 minutes stirring constantly. Peel, core and slice apple, then add to pan. Crush juniper berries and add, then pour over cider and bring to the boil. Cover with a tight-fitting lid and simmer gently for 1 hour. Cool and freeze.

To serve, allow to thaw completely at room temperature and reheat slowly but thoroughly. Add salt and pepper, then stir in brandy.

Lemon Ice Cream

Wonderfully quick and simple, this recipe was given to me by a friend, who was a keen cook and a helpful critic when he ate in my London restaurant.

8 egg yolks
6 oz (185g) sugar
grated peel and juice of 2 lemons
10 fl oz (315 ml) double (heavy) cream

Beat egg yolks in a bowl until creamy. Gradually add sugar and beat until sugar is dissolved and egg mixture is very light and fluffy. Add lemon peel and beat again. In another bowl whip cream until stiff, fold in lemon juice, then fold in yolk mixture. Pour into a container and freeze.

Peppermint Parfait

This recipe will use up some of the egg white left over from the previous recipe.

6 oz (185g) sugar
8 fl oz (250 ml) water
3 egg whites
10 fl oz (315 ml) double (heavy) cream
3-4 drops pure peppermint oil
3-4 drops red food colouring
peppermint liqueur, to serve.

Mix sugar and water together in a heavy-bottomed saucepan, heat gently until sugar is dissolved, then boil hard for 3-5 minutes, watch care-fully, do not allow to darken. Leave aside and keep warm.

Beat egg whites in a bowl until very stiff, then slowly pour in sugar syrup in a thin stream, beating all the time. Leave to cool in the fridge. In another bowl whip cream until stiff, then add peppermint oil and food colouring. When egg whites are cold, blend both mixtures together – this should be the prettiest pale pink. Pour into a container and freeze.

Serve with a drizzle of peppermint liqueur poured over.

The
Spice Cupboard

GOOD PLAIN cooking all year round and spice once a year at Christmas was the general rule of the kitchen from the beginning of the nineteenth century to the mid-twentieth century, when a change occurred.

People began to travel more freely and on return wanted to learn how to cook the subtly-spiced dishes they had eaten abroad, so unlike the hot thick curries cooked at home.

In 1968 a great cookery writer, Claudia Roden, wrote a wonderful cookery book which more surely than anything else spread the gentle art of spice cookery.

It was at this time that I went with my family to live in Turkey. Before I left I wisely bought Claudia Roden's book and she guided me through the spice market of Istanbul where I looked, sniffed, sampled and bought.

It was not until I was settled in my own primitive kitchen, an hour's rough drive from the nearest small town and hundreds of miles from Istanbul that I could begin to practise that art, and then, luckily, I had a teacher: a neighbour and friend came in every day to help me overcome the difficulties of cooking with those unknown ingredients. She shared with me her spices, recipes and knowledge.

Now back home in our own family kitchen I cannot imagine cooking without the contents of my spice cupboard; spice to me is next in value to salt. Like a medieval cook I use a pinch of spice in many dishes both sweet and savoury.

Unfortunately, as I found in my restaurants, people still tend to think of spices as a fiery experience never to be repeated. So I learned to be very discreet with the addition of spices. Only slowly did customers learn that their favourite Senegalese or Kashmir Soup contained the dreaded curry.

Senegalese Soup

This soup is usually chilled or served as a cold summer soup, but it is very good hot and most original.

2 large cooking (tart) apples
4 large eating apples
20 fl oz (625 ml) chicken or vegetable
   stock
1 small onion, sliced
1 tablespoon oil or ½ oz (15g) butter
1 teaspoon curry powder or paste
1 teaspoon ground cumin
1 teaspoon ground coriander
½ teaspoon ground ginger
1 tablespoon chutney
1 tablespoon sugar
1 tablespoon vinegar
10 fl oz (315 ml) plain yogurt
10 fl oz (315 ml) single (light) cream
bunch of fresh mint, chopped

Wipe apples clean, quarter and core, do not peel. Place in a saucepan, add stock, cover and cook until tender, 20-25 minutes. When apples are tender, remove with a slotted spoon, then sieve, or purée in a blender or food processor. Stir in cooking juice. Gently fry onion in butter, do not allow to colour. Add curry powder or paste, spices, chutney, sugar and vinegar, then sieve or purée in blender or food processor. Mix all together in saucepan and bring to the boil. Add yogurt and cream and gently reheat. Do not boil. Add mint to serve.

Kashmir Soup

A delicious, subtly-spiced soup. Garam masala is available in specialist stores and delicatessens (see page 66).

8 oz (250g) good-quality dried apricots
   (darkest colour possible)
20 fl oz (625 ml) cold tea
about 20 fl oz (625ml) thick chicken
   stock
1 tablespoon chopped fresh mint
½ teaspoon of garam masala or
   a pinch of curry powder
salt and pepper
5 fl oz (155 ml) double (heavy) cream
3 fl oz (90ml) medium dry sherry
fresh mint, to garnish

Rinse apricots, then soak overnight in cold tea. The next day, put apricots and tea into a saucepan and simmer until tender, 30-45 minutes. Transfer the mixture to a blender or food processor and purée until smooth. Pour back into a large saucepan and blend in stock, chopped mint, garam masala or curry powder and a good seasoning of salt and pepper. Finally, stir in cream and sherry. If the soup seems too thick, thin slightly with extra chicken stock. Reheat gently, then garnish with chopped mint or float a whole mint leaf on each serving.

Cumin & Sesame Seed Eggs

A favourite lunch in our Turkish kitchen was hard-boiled eggs dipped in a powder of cumin and crushed sesame seeds and salt; a green salad and fresh local bread were all that was needed to accompany them. When we came to eat these eggs at home they tasted less exotic so this recipe evolved.

6 hard-boiled eggs
2 tablespoons olive oil
1 tablespoon wine vinegar
2 oz (60g) curd cheese
1 tablespoon sesame seeds
1 teaspoon ground cumin
salt and pepper, to taste
1 tablespoon toasted sesame seeds,
   to finish

Cut eggs in half lengthwise, remove yolks and place in a bowl with olive oil and vinegar. Beat well, add curd cheese and beat again until smooth. Crush sesame seeds in a pestle and mortar or in a bowl with the flat end of a rolling pin, mix in cumin, then add to egg mixture. Mix well and add salt and pepper. Fill the whites of the eggs with this stuffing. Sprinkle liberally with toasted sesame seeds before serving.

Halibut with Coriander Sauce

This sauce is good with any white fish, it can be made ahead and slowly reheated. Do use whole coriander seeds, their flavour is very delicate.

Serves 4

2 lb (1 kg) halibut steaks or fillet
2 oz (60g) butter

SAUCE
1 oz (30g) butter
2 teaspoons coriander seeds, crushed
    to a coarse powder
juice of ½ lemon
2 egg yolks
2 tablespoons single (light) cream or
    top of the milk
6 fl oz (185 ml) plain yogurt
salt and white pepper, to taste

To cook halibut, gently melt butter in a large frying pan, add fish, cook very slowly and gently until just

cooked, 3-4 minutes each side. If you have very thick steaks or fillets, cook for 4-5 minutes each side. (Fish is too often ruined by over-cooking.) Keep warm.

To make sauce, melt butter in a small saucepan, add coriander seeds and cook for one minute, taking care butter does not burn, then stir in lemon juice and remove from heat. Place egg yolks in a small bowl, beat with a fork, then slowly pour on lemon, butter and coriander mixture, beating all the time. Place cream in saucepan, heat gently, then add yogurt, egg yolk mixture and salt and pepper. This sauce should be just warm, if it gets too hot it will curdle. Pour over fish to serve.

Chicken Tikia

1½ lb (750g) minced chicken
2 cloves of garlic, chopped
2 tablespoons cooking oil
1 teaspoon ground cumin
½ teaspoon coriander
1 teaspoon ground cinnamon
½ teaspoon ground ginger
salt and pepper, to taste

In a bowl combine all ingredients, mixing very thoroughly. Shape into balls about the size of a walnut and grill. They can be fried instead, in 2 tablespoons cooking oil, or barbecued.

Serve with plain boiled rice and a cucumber salad.

Spiced Carrot Loaf

A vegetarian main course. Garam masala is a subtle blend of spices, it can be bought commercially or you can blend your own; most Indian cookery books will give a list of the spices used. It is not generally used on its own, but as a base for the addition of other spices. I like to use it on its own in this dish.

1 medium onion, grated
1 lb (500g) carrots, grated
1 lb (500g) potatoes, grated
6 oz (185g) breadcrumbs
4 eggs
6 fl oz (185 ml) milk
2 teaspoons garam masala
salt and pepper, to taste
2 oz (60g) butter
1 tablespoon toasted sunflower seeds, to finish

Put vegetables and breadcrumbs into a large bowl and mix well. In a separate bowl beat eggs with a fork, then add milk, garam masala, salt and pepper. Stir together well, pour over vegetables and mix thoroughly.

Melt butter in a small saucepan. Line a 2lb (1 kg) loaf tin with greaseproof paper and, using a pastry brush, paint the paper with some of the melted butter. Pour in the carrot mixture, pour over the remaining melted butter and bake for 1 hour at 190°C (375°F/Gas 5). To serve, turn out onto a heated platter, gently remove greaseproof paper and sprinkle with toasted sunflower seeds. I like to serve a cabbage dish to accompany this, spinach is also good.

Spiced Blackcurrant Sorbet

This is made with fresh blackcurrants, it keeps very well and does not lose flavour.

8 fl oz (250 ml) water
13 oz (410g) sugar
1 lb (500g) blackcurrants
½ teaspoon ground allspice
2 egg whites

Gently heat water and 12 oz (375g) of the sugar together in a saucepan until sugar is dissolved, then boil for five minutes. Purée currants in a blender or food processor, then pass through a coarse sieve to remove most of the pips. Mix purée and sugar syrup together with allspice and freeze, until mixture reaches the mushy stage.

Meanwhile, beat egg whites until very stiff in a clean bowl. Slowly add remaining sugar, beating hard. Take soft, mushy currant mixture out of freezer and fold in egg whites. Pour into container and freeze.

Rhubarb & Orange Compote

For all its tart flavour and unusual shape, rhubarb is a splendid fruit, especially if it is used to complement other flavours. This is a delicious version of that usually acid dish 'stewed rhubarb'.

2 lb (1 kg) rhubarb, trimmed and diced
4 tablespoons water
2 oranges
8-12 oz (250-375 g) pale soft brown sugar
1 teaspoon ground cinnamon
¼ teaspoon ground cloves

In a saucepan, preferably stainless steel or enamel, place rhubarb and water, cover tightly and bring to the boil, then simmer very slowly for 20-30 minutes. The rhubarb looks prettier if you can keep the pieces whole. Grate peel of both oranges. When rhubarb is tender, pour into a dish, add sugar, orange peel and spices and gently mix together. Just before serving, peel oranges and slice thinly, cut slices in four and mix with rhubarb.

Cardamon Biscuits (Cookies)

Cardamon is a very subtle spice, much used in Scandinavian cookery. Thin, crisp and delicious, these biscuits (cookies) go particularly well with fruit sorbets.

6 oz (185 g) butter
4 oz (125 g) icing (powdered) sugar
6 cardamon pods, seeds removed
5 oz (155 g) plain (all-purpose) flour
1 teaspoon cornflour (cornstarch)
1 oz (30 g) semolina

In a bowl cream butter and icing sugar together, do not overmix. Pound cardamon seeds in a pestle and mortar or crush in a bowl with the end of a rolling pin, then add to the butter mixture. Sift together flour and cornflour, mix in semolina, then add to butter mixture. Divide dough into three and roll each portion into a log roughly 1 in (2·5 cm) in diameter. Cut in slices ⅛ in (0·3 cm) thick, place on a baking sheet and bake at 190°C (375°F/Gas 5) for 7-12 minutes, until pale golden round the edges. Leave on baking sheet for three minutes. Remove and cool on a wire rack.

Indian Sweetmeats

These are unusual and very delicious. They are an adaptation of a classic Indian recipe given to me by an American cook in Turkey. The original dish would be made with *khoia*, a milk product made by slowly boiling milk until it is a thick creamy paste. Using dried milk may not be authentic but it makes very delicious sweets. They have an elusive fudge-like taste and are called *Barfi Pista* (creamed milk sweets).

1 lb (500g) sugar
30 fl oz (940 ml) water
4 cardamon pods, crushed and seeds
    removed
10 oz (315g) dried milk powder
6 oz (185g) butter
1 tablespoon rose water
3-4 tablespoons milk
20 pistachio nuts, roughly chopped,
    to decorate

Melt sugar in water in a saucepan over a gentle heat. When dissolved, add cardamon seeds, boil for five minutes, then set aside but keep warm.

Place dried milk powder in a bowl. Melt butter in a saucepan, but do not let it get too hot, add rose water and three tablespoons of the milk, then pour onto dried milk powder. Mix well; the mixture should look like pastry at the crumb stage, it should ~ like pastry ~ stick together; if not, add some or all of the extra tablespoon of milk. Press out dough on a pastry board until ½ in (0.5cm) thick. Cut into diamond-shaped lozenges and place on a lightly greased baking sheet. Bake at 190°C (375°F/Gas 5) for 8-10 minutes. Watch very carefully, these milk sweets burn easily. Remove from baking sheet while still warm, place in a serving dish and pour over reserved syrup. Sprinkle with pistachio nuts. They will keep for 2-3 days in the fridge.

The
Spring Kitchen

THE FIRST warm days of early spring are deceptive, for the garden is still bare and we must wait a little longer for the vivid green vegetables and pungent herbs, so delicate when young, to appear; but I am full of hope and expectation for the rhubarb is ready for forcing and small green leaves are showing on the mint and lemon balm.

Spring is not only a time for tasting the first new season's vegetables; it is also a time for using up the remains of late autumn and winter stores.

The thought of the good things to come adds a zest to cooking at this time of year. There is also a certain ease in the kitchen for my load is lighter, the family do not need such solid, filling meals as they did in the heart of winter and, apart from late marmalade-making, the chores of putting up stores for the larder are far away.

The urge to pick and use something from these first spring days is strong and I am tempted by the lemon balm at the back door and pick just a small handful of leaves to flavour some fish or perhaps a carrot soup.

Carrot & Spring Herb Soup

Lemon balm is a common garden herb. It is prolific and will not be harmed if you pick the first early leaves. It goes very well with root vegetables.

1 oz (30g) butter
1½ lb (750g) carrots, chopped
1 medium onion, chopped
1 oz (30g) rice
1 tablespoon chopped fresh lemon balm
2 teaspoons chopped fresh mint
35 fl oz (1.1 litres) white stock or
   bouillon

TO FINISH
a nut of butter
salt and pepper, to taste
6 fl oz (185ml) cream or plain yogurt
   or a mixture of the two

Melt butter in a heavy saucepan, add vegetables and stir-fry gently for five minutes, then add rice and stir-fry for a minute longer. Next add chopped herbs and stock or bouillon, cover, bring to the boil and simmer for 30-45 minutes, until vegetables are very tender. Sieve or put in a blender or food processor to make a fine purée. Reheat, add a nut of butter, salt and pepper, and serve decorated with swirls of cream or yogurt.

Lovage Soup

Lovage has a strong, pungent flavour and is best used young and with discretion ~ this soup is wonderfully stimulating to the palate and can be served hot or cold.

1 oz (30g) butter
1 medium onion, very finely chopped
4 tablespoons finely chopped lovage

15 fl oz (470 ml) white stock or bouillon
20 fl oz (625 ml) milk
6 fl oz (185 ml) double (heavy) cream

Melt butter in a heavy saucepan, add onion and fry very gently until tender but not browned. Add lovage, stir-fry for one minute, then pour in stock or bouillon and cook for 15 minutes. Add milk and bring to the boil, stir in cream and serve.

Marinated Lemon Sole

A very delicate starter. You do need very fresh fish. Ask your fishmonger to fillet them.

3 lemon sole, filleted
2 tablespoons vodka
thinly pared peel of 1 lemon
1 in (2.5 cm) piece of fresh ginger,
    peeled and sliced
6 black peppercorns
juice of 3-4 lemons
crudités, to serve

Skin sole fillets ~ black and white skins must be removed. Cut in half lengthwise, wash gently and pat dry, then place in a large shallow dish and sprinkle with vodka. Slice pared lemon peel into thin strips. Mix with ginger and layer with fish. Crush peppercorns, not too small, and sprinkle over the top. Pour lemon juice over fish. Make sure all the fish is well coated. Cover tightly and leave to marinate overnight in the fridge. Turn fish several times during its marinating to make sure all the fillets get well impregnated with lemon juice. The lemon juice acts as a 'cure' and preserves the fish for 12-24 hours.

To serve, place two pieces of fish on each plate and decorate with a selection of very finely cut crudités, such as carrots, celery and green peppers. Crunchy Sesame Seed Biscuits (see page 29) are good to eat with this dish.

71

Fish Pie with Lemon Balm

This recipe uses old potatoes and the first sprigs of lemon balm. Small in-shore cod is good at this time of year.

2 lb (1 kg) potatoes, peeled
salt and pepper, to taste
2 oz (60g) butter
2½ lb (1.25 kg) cod fillets, skinned
½ onion, roughly chopped
12 fl oz (375ml) milk
2 tablespoons chopped fresh lemon balm
1 tablespoon cornflour (cornstarch)

Boil potatoes in salted water until tender. Strain and mash, beat in butter and a little freshly ground black pepper. Set aside and keep warm. In a shallow pan, poach fillets and onion in milk for 5-6 minutes, then remove fillets from milk and place in a pie dish; discard onion. Sprinkle fish with lemon balm. In a small bowl mix cornflour with two tablespoons of the milk, return to pan with rest of milk and bring to the boil stirring constantly, until sauce is thick. Pour over fish. Carefully cover fish with mashed potato. Place in a moderately hot oven, 200°C (400°F/ Gas 6), and bake for 15-20 minutes. You will only need a salad to accompany this.

Calf's Liver with Chanterelles

A luxury dish with a lovely sauce.

2 oz (60g) dried chanterelles
2 fl oz (60ml) Madeira
1 calf's liver - about 2-2½ lb (1-1.25 kg)
   weight
10 fl oz (315 ml) brown stock
10 fl oz (315 ml) white wine
10 fl oz (315 ml) orange juice
salt and pepper, to taste

In a bowl soak chanterelles in Madeira for ½-1 hour.

In a large flameproof casserole poach liver with stock, wine and orange juice ~ you must be very careful doing this, the liver must only just simmer ~ for 20-30 minutes, depending on how pink you like it. When liver is cooked, carefully place on a warm platter, cover with foil and keep warm. Fast boil stock and reduce by half, add chanterelles and Madeira and simmer for five minutes. Stir in salt and pepper, then pour over liver. Slice when served.

Yogurt Poussin

Corn-fed poussins are rare: this is a good recipe for the less flavourful birds which are more commonly available. It is a good party dish as the birds will not spoil if kept waiting for late guests.

6 small poussins
12 fl oz (375 ml) thick plain yogurt
6 fl oz (185 ml) double (heavy) cream
1 medium onion
1 teaspoon ground turmeric
1 teaspoon ground ginger
12 cardamon pods, seeds removed
   and crushed

Arrange birds in a roasting tin, place in a hot oven, 230°C (450°F/Gas 8), and sear for 6-8 minutes. Meanwhile, combine yogurt and cream in a bowl, add onion and spices and mix well. Remove birds from oven and spoon yogurt and spice mixture over each bird, lower oven temperature to 200°C (400°F/Gas 6) and cook for a further 20-25 minutes, basting frequently, until tender. The length of the cooking time depends on size of poussins.

73

To Roast Easter Lamb

Choose a really good leg of lamb, the best you can afford, spike it with slivers of garlic cut from two or three cloves, and lots of mint. To do this make small incisions in the leg with a long, thin, sharp knife, stuff the garlic and mint into the cuts with your fingers, finally push in a tiny knob of butter.

Roast in a hot oven, 200-220°C (400-425°F/Gas 6-7) for 15 minutes per 1 lb (500g) ~ longer if you like your lamb well cooked.

Rabbit with Lemon & Parsley

Serves 4

4 oz (125g) butter
1 plump tender rabbit, jointed
6 spring onions (scallions), chopped
4 tablespoons chopped fresh parsley
grated peel of 2 lemons
salt and pepper, to taste

Melt butter in a heavy saucepan, add rabbit pieces and fry for 10 minutes, turning frequently. Cover with a tight-fitting lid and cook very slowly until tender, for ¾-1 hour. Five minutes before end of cooking time add spring onions, parsley and lemon peel, salt and pepper.

This is particularly delicious served with pasta.

Pigeons(Squab) in Red Wine Marinade

This unusual recipe has a hot marinade, which we know as 'Frankenstein's tenderiser'. I started using it at a time when I had a Swiss 'helper' in my restaurant, a charming and shy young man whom we unkindly nicknamed Frankenstein! Start two days ahead for this dish as the birds are best if marinated for at least twenty-four hours.

6 pigeons (squab)

MARINADE
2 onions, roughly chopped
2 carrots, chopped
2 oranges, squeezed and peel chopped
10 floz (315 ml) olive or cooking oil
2 cloves garlic, peeled and bruised
2 blades mace
8 allspice
10 lovage seeds
2 bay leaves
1 bottle red wine
salt and pepper, to taste

Make sure your birds are really clean inside. In a very large bowl mix together onions, carrots and orange peel. Add orange juice and 6 floz (185 ml) of the oil and stir well. Add pigeons and mix all together, coating birds with oil and chopped vegetables. Place garlic, spices and bay leaves in a saucepan, pour over red wine and bring to the boil, remove from heat and leave to infuse for 10 minutes. Reheat and pour hot over pigeons and vegetables. Cover with a clean cloth and leave in a cool place for 48 hours, turning frequently.

To cook birds, remove from marinade, do not dry, set aside. Strain marinade into a small saucepan, bring to the boil, remove from heat and set aside to cool. When cool, skim off any fat or oil.

Heat remaining oil in a large frying pan. When hot add pigeons breast-side down and brown for 2-3 minutes on each side. Remove, place in a baking dish and roast in a moderately hot oven, 200°C (400°F/Gas 6), for 20 minutes.

Meanwhile make the sauce. Pour marinade into the frying pan the pigeons have been cooking in, boil and reduce by a third. Add salt and pepper and strain into a sauceboat. If the sauce looks very pale don't be afraid to add a dash of gravy brown, it is quite tasteless.

Buttered cabbage is a good vegetable to accompany the birds.

Swiss Chard

We wait a long time for our spring vegetables. Swiss chard is one of the first to appear. I like to cook this vegetable as two separate dishes: the dark green of the leaves I strip off and cook as spinach; the pale opaque stalks I trim, slice into strips, about 3 in (7.5 cm) long and ½ in (1 cm) wide, steam and toss in butter like asparagus.

Casserole Carrots

A very delicious way to cook new carrots.

2 lb (1 kg) carrots ~ preferably with their green tops still on
2 oz (60 g) butter
salt and pepper, to taste

Top and tail carrots, leaving a small amount of young green at the top, wash well and very lightly scrape.

Place in a deep, flameproof casserole with water to cover and butter, salt and pepper ~ be sparing with the seasoning. Bring to the boil on top of the stove, then cover very tightly and place in the oven at 190°C (315°F/ Gas 5) for 15-20 minutes. If your casserole lid doesn't fit really well make a flour and water paste to seal it with.

Cabbage & Green Pepper (Capsicum)

This is a good way to add extra flavour to white cabbages.

1 medium white cabbage
1 green pepper (capsicum), seeded and chopped
1 oz (30g) butter
3 spring onions (scallions), chopped
salt and pepper, to taste

Shred cabbage very thinly and blanch for 3-4 minutes in boiling, salted water, or steam until cooked but still crisp. Drain and keep warm.

Cook green pepper gently in butter for 4-5 minutes until tender, add spring onions, salt and pepper, mix with the drained cabbage and serve.

Cream Cheese Dessert

This is a wonderfully simple pudding, delicious and ideal for using up last year's jam or jelly before you start again with the new season's fruit.

12 oz (375g) curd cheese
3-4 tablespoons well-flavoured jam or jelly
3 tablespoons white wine
3 egg whites
1 tablespoon sugar
single (light) cream, to serve

Place curd cheese, jam or jelly and white wine in a blender or food processor and blend well together. Alternatively, beat in a bowl with electric beaters.

Beat egg whites in another bowl until very stiff, slowly beat in sugar, then fold egg whites into cheese mixture. Turn into a serving dish and chill for half an hour. Serve with single cream.

Rhubarb Fool

1½ lb (750g) rhubarb
1 tablespoon butter
2 tablespoons water
4 oz (125g) sugar
1 heaped teaspoon cornflour (cornstarch)
10 fl oz (315 ml) milk
3 egg yolks
6 fl oz (185 ml) double (heavy) cream

Top and tail rhubarb and cut into 1 in (2.5 cm) slices.

In a saucepan place butter and water, add rhubarb, cover and simmer for 10-12 minutes, until rhubarb is tender. Pour into a bowl and mix in sugar.

Blend cornflour with a little of the milk in another bowl, add egg yolks and mix together until smooth. Heat remaining milk in a saucepan. When it boils pour over cornflour and egg mixture, mix well and return to saucepan over a very gentle heat, stirring all the time. Cook until custard mixture coats the back of a spoon and cornflour is cooked. Leave to cool, stirring occasionally.

To finish, whip cream in a bowl until thick. Mix rhubarb and custard mixtures together and fold in cream. Chill before serving.

Franzipan Tart

A lovely pudding to follow a light supper on a cool spring evening. This tart recipe fills a 9 in (22.5 cm) flan tin. Use one with a removable base.

PASTRY

2 oz (60g) butter
2 oz (60g) sugar
4 oz (125g) plain (all-purpose) flour, sieved
    sieved

FILLING

2 tablespoons raspberry or apricot jam
4 oz (125g) butter or margarine
4 oz (125g) caster (superfine) sugar
4 eggs
4 oz (125g) ground almonds
¼ oz (15g) plain (all-purpose) flour

Melt butter very slowly in a saucepan, do not allow it to get too hot. Stir in sugar, leave to cool slightly, then add flour. Mix well together and press firmly into a 9 in (22.5 cm) flan tin. Bake blind in a moderately hot oven, 200°C (400°F/Gas 6), for 15 minutes. Cool slightly, then spread with jam.

Cream butter or margarine and sugar in a bowl until light and fluffy, add eggs one by one, beating well in between. Fold in ground almonds and flour. Pour over jam-lined pastry and bake at 190°C (375°F/Gas 5) for 20-25 minutes, until pale golden.

An Easter Cake

This is not a traditional Simnel Cake but a cherry cake with a central layer of marzipan. It is lighter in texture than the spiced Simnel. Start at least four days prior to cooking and make one or two weeks before cutting.

12 oz (375g) glacé cherries
4 tablespoons Kirsch or Kirsch and white wine

ALMOND PASTE
8 oz (250g) ground almonds
10 oz (315g) caster (superfine) sugar
1 egg
few drops of almond essence

CAKE
6 oz (185g) butter
6 oz (185g) sugar
3 eggs
8 oz (250g) self-raising flour, sifted
1 tablespoon ground almonds
4 oz (125g) citrus peel – mixed (candied) peel can be used
1-2 tablespoons apricot or raspberry jam
beaten egg yolk, to glaze

Wash cherries to remove syrup and spread out on absorbent kitchen paper to dry. When dry, cut in half and place in a jar or container with a tight-fitting lid, pour over Kirsch and seal. Leave in a cool, dark place for as many days as you can, turning jar upside down and back several times to ensure all the cherries are marinated. When you come to use the cherries most of the Kirsch should have been absorbed.

To prepare almond paste, mix together almonds and sugar in a bowl. In another bowl lightly beat egg and almond essence together, add egg mixture to almonds and mix well, turn onto a board and knead until smooth. Cut off a third of the paste, roll out to fit an 8 in (20 cm) cake tin, wrap remaining marzipan in plastic wrap and set aside for decorating. Line cake tin with buttered greaseproof paper.

To prepare cake, cream butter and sugar together in a bowl until light and fluffy, add eggs one by one, beating well in between. Using a metal spoon, fold in flour. Strain cherries and add any remaining juice to egg and flour mixture. Sprinkle almonds over cherries and fold into cake mixture. Add peel, mix gently and pour half of mixture into lined cake tin. Make level and place marzipan layer on top; pour on remaining half of mixture and hollow out the centre slightly. Place in a moderate oven, 180°C (350°F/ Gas 4), and bake for 45 minutes, then reduce oven temperature to 160°C (325°F/Gas 3) and bake for a further 1½ -2 hours until firm to the touch.

Remove from oven, rest for 15

minutes, then turn out onto a wire rack, remove paper and cool.

To decorate, divide remaining marzipan into two. Roll out one half to fit top of cake and shape 10-12 eggs from remaining half. Brush top of cake with a thin layer of jam and fit marzipan layer. Decorate the edges with the markings of a fork giving a basket-like pattern, brush with egg yolk and brown under a hot grill. Arrange marzipan eggs around edge, brush tops with egg yolk and brown eggs under the grill. Store cake in an airtight container ~ it will keep up to a month.

The
Summer Kitchen

SUMMER is the start of the harvest of fruits and vegetables. After waiting through the slow-growing spring months, the summer green seems to come suddenly and there is a rush of activity: picking in the garden, cooking and preserving in the kitchen.

It is a time both of frustration and excitement. I have to pick, to market, also to cook for the family yet I must escape to sit in the garden, for who wants to spend every lovely day slaving over the proverbial hot stove? It needs all one's enthusiasm now to get through the summer kitchen chores, so as both to eat fresh foods and to preserve this summer harvest at its best.

But summer meals are a special delight, particularly when eaten out of doors beneath our beautiful blue wistaria. The food can be simple, light and quickly prepared from fast-cooking fresh ingredients, such as new peas, young tender broad beans cooked whole or salads of cut-and-come-again lettuces, sweet and refreshing with a herb vinaigrette.

Now is the time to start experimenting with herbs: try tomatoes with mint, dill with beans and basil with fish or poultry.

Not only do baskets in the cool larder groan with home produce, but shops and markets are overflowing with apricots, peaches and nectarines. The first of the new season's pears arrive, scented and succulent, oozing with juice and, though it is extravagant, I like to use them to make a chilled soup, delicately flavoured with tarragon.

Pear & Tarragon Soup

This most subtle of summer soups I usually serve cold as it tends to be a little too sweet if served hot.

30 fl oz (940 ml) chicken or mild vegetable stock
2-3 sprigs tarragon, finely chopped
4-6 ripe pears, depending on size and flavour
2 teaspoons wine vinegar
6 fl oz (185 ml) plain yogurt
2 tablespoons double (heavy) cream
salt and pepper, to taste
4 chives, snipped

Bring stock to the boil in a saucepan with tarragon, then remove from heat. Wash, quarter and core pears, do not peel. Place in a blender or food processor with vinegar and process to a fine thick purée, add to stock, then leave to cool. Mix yogurt and cream together, blend with pear mixture, add salt and pepper. To serve, pour into bowls and sprinkle with a little of the chives.

Poppy Seed Pancakes

A great summer favourite: the poppy seeds add an unusual texture that complements the smoked salmon filling. Poppy seeds are available at delicatessens and health food shops. I make these pancakes in a 6 inch (15 cm) frying pan.

Basic pancake mixture: omitting cinnamon, ginger and sugar, see page 30.

1 oz (30 g) poppy seeds

FILLING

6-8 oz (185-250 g) smoked salmon pieces
6 fl oz (185 ml) sour cream OR
3 fl oz (90 ml) plain yogurt
3 fl oz (90 ml) double (heavy) cream } -
    mixed together
2 spring onions (scallions), green and
    white, finely chopped
freshly ground black pepper
lemon wedges, to decorate

Make up pancake batter following the Ginger Pancakes recipe on page 30. Pour pancake batter into pan as directed in pancake recipe. When batter covers bottom of pan sprinkle liberally with poppy seeds; cook and turn in the normal way. When all your pancakes are cooked cover with plastic wrap and store in the fridge until required.

To make the filling, trim and chop smoked salmon pieces carefully. Stir into sour cream or yogurt mixture, add spring onions and pepper. Mix well. Cover and keep in fridge until needed.

To serve, place a heaped teaspoon of the filling on each pancake, fold in half and decorate with lemon wedges.

Cucumber Mousse with Crab

1 cucumber, peeled
3 tablespoons white wine
½ oz (15g) powdered gelatine
1 teaspoon chopped chives
1 teaspoon chopped dill
2 tablespoons plain yogurt
salt and pepper, to taste
1 large crab or 2 small
2 tablespoons vinaigrette
1 egg white
unpeeled cucumber slices, to decorate

Grate cucumber into a colander, then place a small plate on cucumber and a weight on top. Place colander in a bowl and leave to drain for an hour. Pour drained cucumber juice into a small saucepan, add white wine and heat through. Remove from heat and sprinkle in gelatine, stir until dissolved. In a bowl mix together grated cucumber, herbs, yogurt, salt and pepper, then mix in gelatine mixture. Leave in the fridge for 30-45 minutes or until mixture begins to set.

Meanwhile prepare crab. Separate brown meat from white, add 1 tablespoon of the vinaigrette to brown meat and mix well. Add remaining tablespoon to white meat and toss gently. When cucumber mixture begins to set, whip egg white until stiff and fold into the mixture. Place a layer of brown crab meat in the bottoms of six small ramekins, half-fill with cucumber mousse, then add a layer of white meat, top up with mousse, then chill. Serve decorated with very thin slices of unpeeled cucumber.

Minted Prawns with Avocado & Melon

A very pretty summer starter. If using frozen prawns weigh after defrosting and draining.

8 oz (250g) cooked and peeled prawns
2 tablespoons vinaigrette
2 tablespoons chopped fresh mint
salt, if desired
1 small ripe melon
2 tablespoons lemon juice
2 avocados
fresh mint leaves, to decorate

Toss together prawns, vinaigrette and mint in a bowl. Salt may not be needed as the vinaigrette is usually salted. Cover and leave to marinate in the fridge for 1-2 hours. Just before serving, slice melon into wedges and peel, slice wedges crosswise and set aside. Pour lemon juice into a shallow dish. Peel, halve and slice avocados lengthwise, dipping each slice immediately in lemon juice to prevent browning. When all avocado is sliced assemble the dish. Arrange a row of overlapping avocado on each individual plate, then a row of melon. Complete with a little heap of prawn mixture and decorate with mint leaves. This looks very cool and appetising.

Noisettes of Lamb with Mint Béarnaise

This is my favourite way of cooking lamb, it looks pretty and the mint béarnaise is so much nicer than a tart mint sauce.

Ask your butcher to bone out a loin of lamb for you, or you can do it yourself with a sharp knife – it is not difficult. This gives you a long fillet of lamb, very lean and tender. You could use shoulder fillets, which are much cheaper, but rather too fatty for this dish.

6 tablespoons white wine

6 tablespoons wine vinegar

1 slice of onion

2 sprigs of mint

3 peppercorns

9 oz (280g) butter, softened

3 egg yolks

1 tablespoon chopped fresh mint

salt and pepper, to taste

2 tablespoons olive oil

1 fillet of loin from the rack weighing
   1¾ - 2 lb (875g - 1kg), cut into
   noisettes ¾-1 in (2-2.5cm) thick

mint sprigs, to serve

In a small saucepan put wine, vinegar, onion, mint sprigs, peppercorns and 1 oz (30g) of the butter, boil until reduced by two-thirds. Remove from the heat.

Place egg yolks in a bowl that will fit over a saucepan of simmering water or in the top of a double boiler. Beat yolks with a wire whisk, then place bowl over the hot water and strain in wine and vinegar. Beat well, then very slowly add remaining butter, about a teaspoon at a time, beating it in thoroughly. (This is like making a mayonnaise.) When all butter is used up, add chopped mint and salt and pepper. This sauce should be served warm. Do not boil.

In a large heavy pan heat oil and very quickly fry noisettes for two minutes each side – more if you like them well done, though this lamb is best 'pink'. Serve with a little sprig of mint on each plate and hand mint béarnaise separately.

Guinea Fowl with Fresh Apricots

This is a very delicate dish. One large guinea fowl should feed four. Guinea fowl can be dry; pot roasting avoids this.

1 oz (30g) butter

1 guinea fowl

6 chives

4 sprigs lemon balm

1 lb (500g) fresh apricots, halved and stoned, kernels reserved

4 tablespoons white wine

2 tablespoons brandy

2 tablespoons white stock

salt and pepper, to taste

1 tablespoon slivered almonds, toasted

Melt butter in a casserole and gently brown guinea fowl all over, add herbs, half the apricots and the kernels of the stones, cover, place in a moderately hot oven, 200°C (400°F/Gas 6), and cook for 45 minutes or until tender.

In a saucepan gently poach remaining apricot halves in wine, brandy and stock for 8-10 minutes until tender. Set aside. When guinea fowl is done, place on a serving dish, arrange poached apricots around it and keep warm. Skim fat off juices in casserole and strain into brandy and stock. Sieve herbs and apricots used to flavour guinea fowl, add to gravy, then add salt and pepper. Reheat and pour into a gravy boat to serve, or pour over the guinea fowl. Sprinkle fowl with toasted almonds.

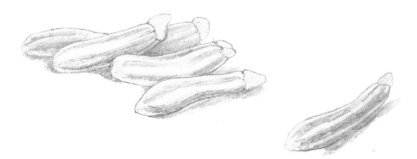

Minted Courgettes (Zucchini)

2 tablespoons oil

1 oz (30g) butter

1½ lb (750g) courgettes (zucchini), cut into ¼ in (0.5 cm) slices

2 tablespoons chopped fresh mint

salt and pepper, to taste

Heat oil and butter in a heavy pan with a tight-fitting lid, toss in courgettes, stir well to coat with oil and butter, then cover tightly and sweat for 5-6 minutes, shaking pan constantly to prevent burning. Two minutes before they are cooked, add mint, salt and pepper. Serve at once.

Strawberry Mallow

This is a dish for the first few strawberries of the season.

8 oz (250g) strawberries
20 marshmallows
2 tablespoons white wine
6 fl oz (185ml) double (heavy) cream
grated chocolate, to finish

Hull strawberries and wash if necessary, halve and set aside. Cut marshmallows into quarters. Pour wine into a saucepan, add marshmallows and melt very gently over a low heat. Cool a little. Whip cream, fold marshmallows into cream, then add strawberries. Pour into little glass dishes or ramekins. To serve, dust with grated chocolate.

Nectarine Tart

Fresh, ripe nectarines are so delicious on their own that it seems a pity to cook them, but this tart is very special.

PASTRY BASE
2½ oz (75g) butter
2½ oz (75g) sugar
5½ oz (170g) plain (all-purpose) flour

FILLING
4-6 nectarines, depending on size
2 whole eggs
2 egg yolks
1 oz (30g) caster (superfine) sugar
5-6 fl oz (155-185ml) double (heavy) cream
2 teaspoons orange flower water
2 oz (60g) ground almonds

Make and bake pastry in a 9in (22.5cm) flan tin as described in the method for Franzipan Tart, see page 78.

In a bowl combine eggs, egg yolks and sugar, stir with a wooden spoon until mixture is very smooth, do not beat. Stir in cream and orange flower water. Peel nectarines; if properly ripe they will peel easily, if skins seem difficult, drop for a minute or two into boiling water. Halve, remove stones and slice fruit carefully.

Leaving pastry case in flan tin, line bottom of pastry with ground almonds, pressing down firmly. Layer nectarines in overlapping circles until the whole base is neatly covered. Place flan tin on a baking sheet and very carefully pour on the egg and cream mixture; the mixture slowly seeps through the fruit, so keep topping up. Bake in a moderate oven, 180°C (350°F/Gas 4), for 35-40 minutes, until custard is set. Should the top begin to brown place a piece of foil over tart, heat-reflecting side upwards.

Honey Nougat Ice Cream

This has a lovely nougat flavour without any of the chewiness.

2 oz (60g) hazelnuts
2 oz (60g) glacé cherries, quartered
2 oz (60g) angelica, chopped
4 tablespoons honey
4 eggs, separated
10 fl oz (315 ml) double (heavy) cream
1 tablespoon rose water

Toast hazelnuts over a medium heat in a clean, dry frying pan. When they are nicely brown, turn them out onto a sheet of absorbent kitchen paper, cool slightly, then rub their skins off while still warm. Leave to cool, then crush in a pestle and mortar, keeping them in fairly large pieces. Mix with cherries and angelica, then set aside.

In a small saucepan melt two table-spoons of the honey. Beat egg yolks in a bowl, pour on hot honey and beat until light and fluffy. Place in the freezer for 30 minutes until beginning to go firm round the edges. In saucepan heat last two tablespoons of honey, remove from heat but keep warm. Beat egg whites until stiff, then slowly drizzle in warm honey, beating all the time. Place in freezer while you beat up cream with rose water until stiff. Remove containers from freezer. Fold fruit and nuts into egg yolk mixture, then fold in cream and rose water; lastly fold in egg white mixture. Pour into a con-tainer and freeze. I like to freeze this in a long shallow container and serve it cut in slices like real nougat. Accompany with Lacy Biscuits.

Lacy Biscuits (Cookies)

Makes about 20 biscuits (Cookies).

2 oz (60g) butter
2 oz (60g) golden (corn) syrup
1 tablespoon caster (superfine) sugar
2 oz (60g) plain (all-purpose) flour, sifted
2 oz (60g) slivered or toasted almonds

Lightly butter a baking sheet. Melt butter in a saucepan over a low heat. Remove

from heat and blend in golden syrup. Stir in sugar, flour and almonds. When well blended, drop by salt-spoonfuls onto baking sheet – space well apart as they spread! Bake in a moderately hot oven, 200°C (400°F/Gas 6) until pale golden, 6-10 minutes. Allow to cool slightly before lifting carefully off with a palette knife. Cool on a wire rack.

The Hamper

THE MERE *sight of a hamper makes me want to picnic, even in the depths of winter. There is a wonderful feeling of escape, eating food in the open away from home. Appetites are keen and everything tastes so much better outdoors.*

Everybody has a dream picnic place: a desert island with a warm blue sea to swim in; a ski picnic with perfect powder snow and hot alpine sun; a secret picnic in deep pine woods, dark and resin-scented; a smugglers' cove found on a rocky shoreline, filled with memories of a brandy trail; or perhaps tea in the garden beneath a shady tree. My own picnic memories are many and varied, all happy: on a rock near a waterfall, the cool spray damping our clothes; tea in autumn stubble fields after blackberry picking; roasting fish on an old sheet of tin on a Turkish shore with the fishermen, and many more. Even car picnics on long journeys I find fun.

Barbecuing is a simple way of out-door eating. Barbecued meat, baked potatoes and a fresh salad make the simplest meal imaginable and if you like you can eat it off paper plates and throw them away afterwards, and have no more extra work than the tossing of the salad.

'What a bother', friends say when they hear I am preparing for yet another picnic. But it's no bother, it's a pleasure and everybody always helps with picnic preparation. If you give large picnics you will most probably find that your guests will offer to help and bring a dish along but do arrange who is to bring what.

I have tried to give recipes that are simple and not too time-consuming to prepare. I always tuck in a few extra goodies, for appetites are not only keener but larger in the open air.

Avgolemono

A special summer soup, cool and lemony.

40 fl oz (1.25 litres) chicken stock – a
     good strong stock is best
4 eggs
juice of 1 large lemon
salt and pepper, to taste
1 tablespoon fresh basil leaves,
     roughly chopped

Bring stock to the boil in a saucepan.
Beat eggs until frothy in a large bowl
and add lemon juice. When stock

boils, pour onto egg and lemon
mixture, return to pan and reheat
very gently, taking care not to let
it boil or the eggs and lemon will
curdle. Season with salt and pepper.
Serve hot or cold, sprinkled with
basil.

Try adding a freshly-poached egg
to each serving for a summer
lunch in the garden. Follow it with
bread and cheese, a salad and fresh
fruit.

Stuffed Tomatoes

A not impossible picnic dish if you
prepare them this way.

6 large tomatoes
salt and pepper, to taste
6 eggs
2 oz (60g) butter
3 tablespoons single (light) cream
2 tablespoons mayonnaise
2 tablespoons fresh herbs, e.g. chives
     and parsley, dill and spring onions
     (scallions) or basil on its own
sprigs of fresh herbs, to decorate

Slice tops off tomatoes, scoop out and
discard seeds and some of the flesh.
Sprinkle with a little salt and turn

upside down to drain while you
prepare the egg stuffing.

Break eggs into a bowl and mix
well with a fork. In a heavy saucepan
melt butter, add cream, salt and
pepper. Pour in eggs and cook very
slowly, stirring all the time, until
thick and creamy, do not overcook
otherwise they will go watery.
Remove from heat and leave to
cool. When cold, add mayonnaise
and herbs. Fill tomatoes with this
mixture and decorate with fresh
herbs. If you are going to eat these
away from home at the picnic
site the tomatoes transport very
well packed in a plastic container.

Rabbit Terrine

This is a lovely summery terrine, the dill gives the rabbit a fresh, delicate taste. If I am going to turn out a terrine I always line the dish with foil first, then follow with the bacon, etc., this makes it much easier.

1 lb (500g) boned rabbit meat
1 lb (500g) belly pork (fresh pork sides), not too fat
3 fl oz (90ml) dry white wine
1 clove garlic
2 tablespoons chopped fresh dill
salt and pepper, to taste
6 oz (185g) streaky bacon

Cut 8 oz (250g) rabbit and 8 oz (250g) pork into strips, using the best pieces. Marinate in wine for 2-3 hours or overnight in the fridge. Mince remaining rabbit and pork with garlic and mix well together. Add wine from strips, dill, salt and pepper. Line a terrine or a 2 lb (1 kg) loaf tin with streaky bacon, leaving ends overlapping tin. Fill alternately with layers of mince and strips of rabbit and pork, finishing with a layer of mince. Fold over bacon ends, cover with foil, place in a bain marie and cook for 1½-2 hours in a very cool oven, 120°C (250°F/Gas ½). Test with a skewer, if the juices run pink, the terrine needs further cooking. When cooked, remove from water bath, leave to cool a little for 15-20 minutes, then press lightly with a weight and leave overnight. Turn out or carry to the picnic in the terrine.

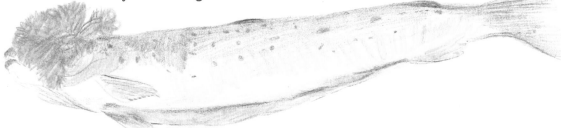

Smoked Trout Pâté

It is easier to make this quick and simple pâté than to carry the fish to the picnic.

2 smoked trout, boned and skinned
6 oz (185g) curd cheese
8 chives, chopped
1 tablespoon Pernod
salt and pepper, to taste

Place trout in a food processor, add curd cheese, chives, Pernod, salt and pepper and blend for as short a time as possible. Pack into a small terrine or individual pots and chill. Serve with a fennel salad and brown bread and butter.

Chicken in a Pancake

This is a party picnic dish, the combination of flavours is cool and refreshing, and, should the weather let you down so that you eat it at home, the dish doesn't look like sad picnic fare. It could be served hot by microwave users. I used to serve it at my restaurant and it was very popular.

Basic pancake mixture, omitting cinnamon, ginger and sugar, see page 30.

FILLING
2 cups cold cooked chicken
1 cup green grapes, seedless if
      possible, otherwise seeded
½ teaspoon curry paste
2 tablespoons plain yogurt
2 tablespoons double (heavy) cream
4 tablespoons mayonnaise
1 bunch chives
1 bunch fresh tarragon
salt and pepper, to taste
tarragon sprigs and a few grapes,
      to garnish

Make 6-8 large pancakes following the Ginger Pancakes recipe on page 30. Place all filling ingredients in a bowl and mix well together. To assemble, place a portion of the filling on each pancake, roll up and decorate with a sprig of tarragon and a few whole grapes.

If you are eating these pancakes away from home, it is better to assemble them at your picnic site, otherwise they may be soggy. Pack filling in a box and wrap pancakes in plastic wrap.

Cheese, Tomato & Basil Quiche

This tart is made with curd cheese which is mild enough to allow the basil and tomato flavours to dominate. It is also rather nicer cold than the usual hard cheeses used in quiches. This is a large tart for eight to ten people.

PASTRY

1 lb (500g) plain (all-purpose) flour
salt and pepper, to taste
9 oz (280g) butter
2 egg yolks or use whole eggs
1-2 tablespoons milk

FILLING

1 lb (500g) tomatoes, not too small
1 large bunch of basil
12 oz (375g) curd cheese
2 whole eggs
2 egg yolks
2 tablespoons cream
a few lettuce leaves

Make pastry case first. Sieve flour, salt and pepper into a large bowl. Cut butter into cubes, add to flour and rub in with the fingertips until mixture looks like breadcrumbs. Beat eggs or egg yolks and milk together with a fork and add to flour and butter mixture. Using fingers, draw flour into eggs and bind together, pressing dough against sides of bowl until you have a smooth surface. Flatten ball of dough a little with the hands, place in a polythene bag and leave in the fridge for 30 minutes. On a lightly-floured work surface, roll dough out into a circle $\frac{1}{8}$ in (0.3 cm) thick and press into a 10 in (25 cm) quiche tin. Prick base with a fork and line with greaseproof paper, sprinkle with dried peas or beans to weight it down. Bake pastry case in a hot oven, 220°C (425°F/Gas 7), for 15 minutes, remove peas and greaseproof paper and bake for a further 4-5 minutes. Set aside while making filling.

Wash tomatoes and slice, not too thinly, sprinkle lightly with salt and leave on absorbent kitchen paper to drain.

In a blender or food processor purée basil leaves, add cheese, eggs and egg yolks, cream, salt and pepper and purée again. Line pastry case with lettuce leaves, pour in cheese mixture and top with sliced tomatoes.

Bake in a moderately hot oven, 190°C (375°F/Gas 5), for 40-50 minutes.

Picnic Beans

This Turkish recipe keeps well and can be eaten hot or cold. The children passed my kitchen window on their way to school carrying little tin pails of these beans, cold, for their lunch. This is an excellent recipe for using up a sudden glut of beans in the garden. It keeps in the fridge and is very good with hard-boiled eggs.

4 tablespoons olive oil
1 medium onion, finely chopped
1 clove garlic, chopped
1 lb (500g) ripe tomatoes, chopped
1 tablespoon tomato purée
salt and pepper, to taste
1½ lb (750g) French (green) beans, topped and tailed

In a saucepan place olive oil, add onion and garlic and cook gently for 5-8 minutes. Add tomatoes and cook for 2 minutes. Add tomato purée, mix well, stir in salt and pepper and lastly add beans. Stir gently over a low heat until beans are well coated with tomato mixture. Cover tightly and cook for 10-12 minutes, depending on age of beans and how crisp you like your vegetables. Serve hot or cold.

Melon with Summer Fruits

This is best prepared in advance to let the fruits absorb the liqueur. If you want it to travel, prepare the fruits, leave to marinate and fill the shell at the picnic. This is a nice contribution to bring to somebody else's picnic; it is a pudding people expect to eat at home, not in a cornfield.

1 medium-sized melon
8 oz (250g) strawberries and raspberries, or other soft fruits
4 tablespoons Cointreau
1 tablespoon chopped fresh mint
few raspberries and strawberries, to decorate

Slice top off melon. Remove seeds and most of flesh. Discard seeds and chop flesh into small cubes. Hull strawberries and pick over raspberries or other soft fruit. Place fruit in a bowl, add Cointreau and mint, mix gently, cover and leave to marinate for several hours. To serve, fill melon shell with marinated fruits and juice, replace top and decorate with a few strawberries and raspberries.

Summer Fruit Cake

This is really only a basic butter sponge mixture with fresh fruit added to it. It makes a lovely moist cake that travels easily. Make and eat on the same day.

4 oz (125g) butter, softened
4 oz (125g) sugar
4 eggs
4 oz (125g) self-raising flour
1 lb (500g) fresh soft fruit, e.g. raspberries, redcurrants or blackberries

Line two 9 in (22.5cm) sponge tins with buttered greaseproof paper. In a bowl cream butter and sugar together until light and fluffy. Add eggs one by one, beating well in between. Gently fold in flour, then soft fruit. Pour into prepared tins and bake at 180°C (350°F/Gas 4) for 25-30 minutes until firm to the touch.

If you are going to eat this cake at home sandwich the two layers together with 6 fl oz (185ml) whipped cream, flavoured with 1 tablespoon raspberry liqueur. To take it with you, fill with some homemade raspberry jam, pack in a cake tin and serve at the picnic in slices to eat with fingers.

Picnic Punch

This looks pretty and tastes wonderful.

2 lb (1kg) raspberries
juice of 4 oranges
10 fl oz (315 ml) water
1 bottle white wine
6 fl oz (185 ml) brandy

Place raspberries, orange juice and water in a liquidizer and process. Strain through a sieve. Mix with white wine and brandy and chill. Transport in vacuum flasks.

The Autumn Kitchen

THE DREAMY season of 'mists and mellow fruitfulness' — and how beautiful these early autumn mornings are. Autumn was traditionally the time of year when the kitchen was bustling with activity as the harvest was preserved for future eating.

We live in a time of abundance and need no longer spend the lovely autumn days in the kitchen preserving foods that were once essential for healthy winter eating. Yet even in these days of frozen, freeze-dried and excellent canned foods, it is surprising to discover that most of us still have an instinctive, squirrel-like urge which dictates that we put aside a hoard, no matter how small, of the best goodies for the leaner winter months and for present-giving.

At the same time we can take advantage of the harvest to eat and enjoy ripe autumn produce at its very best.

There are field mushrooms as big as plates and hedgerows full of berries ~ you may even know where to find wild plums, quite unlike any other plum you've ever tasted. The first home-grown apples are being sold by the roadside. Look out for fresh walnuts, delicious eaten straight from their shells with cheese. Sweet chestnuts appear now: gather your own, they are easy to find in town and country. Roast them in the fire and eat them straightaway.

Autumn storms may limit the choice of fresh fish in the markets, but shellfish are good and the first sweet mussels arrive now. The summer green vegetables are fast dying off but cabbage is excellent with game and there will be plenty of that: grouse is a luxury but partridge, pheasant and hare are all available too.

It is hot soup time again; a great favourite is Fennel Soup made from the last of the Florence fennel bulbs before the frost gets them.

Fennel Soup

1 oz (30g) butter
1 small onion, chopped
4 fennel bulbs (if very large use 3),
    chopped
30 fl oz (940 ml) chicken or vegetable
    stock
10 fl oz (315ml) milk
6 fl oz (185 ml) single (light) cream
salt and pepper, to taste
1 tablespoon Pernod

In a saucepan melt the butter, add onion

and fennel and cook gently over a low heat for 10 minutes, stirring all the time. Pour on stock, cover and simmer for 30-45 minutes, until quite tender. Remove from the heat and purée in a blender or food processor. Return to saucepan, reheat, stir in milk and cream, salt, pepper and Pernod, heat through, then serve straightaway.

This soup is so delicious I serve it alone and undecorated.

Stuffed Mushrooms

6 large mushrooms
10 fl oz (315ml) white stock, or stock and
    white wine
2 spring onions (scallions), chopped
2 oz (60g) cooked ham, chopped
6 oz (185g) curd cheese
2 egg yolks
1 teaspoon chopped fresh herbs, e.g.
    basil, thyme or marjoram, or a
    mixture
salt and pepper, to taste
sprigs of parsley, to decorate

Butter an ovenproof dish large enough to hold the mushrooms. Clean mushrooms with a damp cloth, it should not be necessary to peel them.

Remove stalks and reserve. Place mushroom caps and stock in a shallow pan, bring to the boil and poach for 2-3 minutes on each side. Drain on absorbent kitchen paper. Place mushroom stalks, spring onions, ham, curd cheese and egg yolks in a blender or food processor and blend together for as short a time as possible, then stir in herbs, salt and pepper. Arrange mushrooms in prepared dish and fill each one with curd cheese mixture. Place in hot oven, 220°C (425°F/Gas 7), and cook for 8-12 minutes until stuffing is bubbling hot. Decorate with sprigs of parsley and serve at once.

Tapénade

8 oz (250g) black olives, stoned
8 anchovies
2 fl oz (60ml) olive oil
2 tablespoons brandy

Place all ingredients in a blender or food processor and blend until smooth. Pot in small clean jars, cover and store in a cool place: the fridge is best. Use to flavour white stews or to make this delicious starter.

Tapénade Pâté

4 oz (125g) tapénade
6 oz (185g) curd cheese
4 hard-boiled eggs
2 tablespoons single (light) cream, or
   white wine
½ clove garlic
salt and pepper, to taste

Place all ingredients in a blender or food processor and blend for as short a time as possible. Spoon pâté into a pretty dish. Serve with hot brown toast and lots of olives, sliced tomatoes and pickled dill cucumbers. Delicious.

Mussels with Juniper Sauce

For a main course dish for six people I would buy three pints of mussels or allow twelve per person.

1 tablespoon oil

1 onion

2 bay leaves

10 fl oz (315 ml) white wine

3 pints fresh, thoroughly cleaned mussels or 72 frozen mussels, defrosted

2 oz (60 g) butter

6 juniper berries, crushed

6 fl oz (185 ml) double (heavy) cream

1 tablespoon brandy

salt and pepper, to taste

chopped fresh parsley, to serve

Place oil in a large saucepan, add half the onion and the bay leaves and cook gently for 2-3 minutes. Add wine and bring to the boil, then add some of the mussels, cover and cook for 2-3 minutes. You will not be able to cook all the mussels at once. They will open when they are cooked. Discard any that don't.

When cooked remove to a plate to drain until cool enough to handle. Cook remainder the same way. Take mussels out of their shells and keep warm while you make the sauce.

Strain juices that mussels were cooked in and reserve: you should have about 6 fl oz (185 ml) left.

Chop the remaining half onion. Melt butter in a saucepan, add onion and cook very gently until tender, 8-10 minutes. Add juniper berries and strained stock, boil fast for 5 minutes, then add cream, brandy, salt and pepper. Pour over mussels, sprinkle with parsley and serve.

Marinated Smoked Haddock (Finnan Haddie)

A piece of fillet is best for this, so that you can slice it like smoked salmon. Choose the pale undyed fish as it is much more delicate in flavour. Ask the fishmonger to leave the skin on, it makes the slicing easier.

1 lb (500g) smoked haddock (Finnan Haddie)

3 oranges

3 tablespoons brandy

1 clove garlic, sliced

6 peppercorns, lightly crushed

Start a day ahead. Wash fish in cold water, pat dry. Grate 1 teaspoon of orange peel from one of the oranges, squeeze juice from all three into a bowl and stir in brandy. Add garlic and peppercorns, then pour into a shallow dish. Place fish, skin-side uppermost, in marinade, cover with a piece of greaseproof paper and weight lightly. Place in the fridge and leave for twenty-four hours. To serve, slice as thinly as possible, accompany with brown bread and butter and an orange-flavoured homemade mayonnaise lightened with a little plain yogurt.

Lamb with Aubergine (Eggplant)

This is a lovely dish with a very subtle, smoky flavour. It was a great favourite in my restaurant and makes a lovely dinner party dish — nobody can ever guess how it is made. Make it a day ahead and reheat well to serve.

2 large or 4 medium aubergines (egg-plants) — large are best for this dish

1 leg of lamb, about 4 lb (2 kg) in weight

4 fl oz (125 ml) olive oil

2 cloves garlic, chopped

8 fl oz (250 ml) thick plain yogurt

8 fl oz (250 ml) double (heavy) cream

salt and pepper, to taste

1 tablespoon chopped fresh coriander

Grill aubergines or toast them over a naked flame until their skins are black all over and starting to blister; plunge into a bowl of cold water and very carefully peel off skins, taking care not to leave any charred pieces. Place in a colander, press lightly with the hands and leave to drain.

Trim lamb and remove from the bone, cut into cubes 1½-2 in (4-5 cm) square. Pour olive oil into a large flameproof casserole, heat gently and add lamb and garlic. Gently cook lamb for 20 minutes, stirring well to make sure that all meat is coated with oil and evenly cooked. Cover casserole with a tight-fitting lid, lower the heat and simmer very slowly for 30 minutes, checking occasionally to make sure meat is not burning. After 30 minutes, mash aubergines with a fork and add to meat, with yogurt, cream and a little salt and pepper. This dish needs very little salt, the aubergines seem to have a saltiness of their own. Mix well, bring to the boil, lower the heat and again cook very slowly for a further 30 minutes or until meat is tender. Sprinkle with coriander and serve.

I always accompany this with bulgar wheat.

Bulgar Wheat with Tomatoes

A good dish for a dinner party, for it cooks by itself while you enjoy apéritifs with your guests. The cracked wheat is cooked and served like rice and to my mind is very much nicer. You need a heavy saucepan with a really tight-fitting lid for this and fresh tomatoes should be used.

4 oz (125g) butter
1 lb (500g) bulgar wheat
20 fl oz (625 ml) water ~ you may
    need a little more
salt and pepper, to taste
1 lb (500 g) tomatoes, skinned and
    chopped

Melt butter in a heavy pan, add bulgar wheat and stir-fry over a gentle heat for 8-10 minutes, then pour on water and add salt and pepper. Cover tightly and simmer over a very low heat for 10-15 minutes, checking occasionally to see that bulgar wheat does not get too dry. If it does, add a little extra water. Add tomatoes and stir in gently, leave only just on the heat, or on an asbestos mat, for a further 30 minutes.

Fennel with Celery

This dish uses two strongly-flavoured vegetables. It is a wonderful combination and seems to me to bring out the best in both.

4 fennel bulbs
1 head of celery
salt and pepper,
    to taste
3-4 oz (90-125g)
    butter
1 tablespoon chopped
    fresh parsley

Trim vegetables and slice into chunks. Place in a saucepan and boil quickly in salted water for 6-8 minutes, then drain well and return to pan. Add butter, cover and sweat for 5 minutes, remove lid and simmer for a further 5-8 minutes, then add parsley and pepper, toss and serve.

Sweet & Sour Baby Onions

Pickling onions are used here. They are horrible to peel but delicious to eat like this. All sorts of advice is given for peeling without tears ~ I just hope for the best and try not to weep excessively: the dish is worth the tears!

1½ - 2 lb (750g - 1 kg) pickling onions
salt, to taste
3 oz (90g) butter
2 tablespoons soft brown sugar
1 tablespoon wine vinegar
a good pinch of ground cloves
2 tablespoons currants

Peel onions, place in a saucepan, add salt, cover with boiling water and boil till tender, 10-15 minutes. Drain. Melt butter in a heavy pan, add brown sugar, vinegar, cloves, onions and currants, then cook for 10 minutes, stirring to prevent sugar burning. Serve hot.

Pear Tart

Using the recipe on page 78 for the pastry, and the egg and cream filling from the Nectarine Tart (page 87) you can make a delicious pear tart. Line pastry with a sprinkling of slivered almonds, peel and cut some pears in half, lengthwise, then slice across in neat thin slices. Lay the slices carefully on the almonds, keeping half pear shapes although the pears are sliced. Fill the tart, then pour round the egg and cream filling and bake as for Nectarine Tart. Sprinkle with pear liqueur just before serving.

I like this tart best when it is served warm.

Try plum tart cooked this way; cut some plums in half, remove stones, arrange cut side up in circles to cover the pastry base and fill each half with a blanched almond, dust with one to two tablespoons of sugar, pour round egg and cream filling (you may not need all of it this time) and bake. This tart looks very pretty and it is amazing how many people are fooled into thinking you have cooked the plums with their stones still in.

Plum & Walnut Kissel

Not a dish of stewed fruit but a very delicious dessert, simple to make and fine enough for a feast.

20 fl oz (625ml) red wine
1½ lb (750g) plums, halved and stoned
2 tablespoons cornflour (cornstarch)
4-6 oz (125-185g) sugar
4 oz (125g) walnuts, roughly chopped

TO SERVE
whipped cream
biscuits (cookies)

Heat wine in a saucepan and carefully poach plum halves in batches for 10-15 minutes each until tender, remove from wine with a slotted spoon and drain. Allow to cool. In a bowl mix cornflour with cool, drained juice, return to saucepan with wine, add sugar and stir over a low heat until juice thickens and becomes clear. Add walnuts and cook for 5 minutes, then pour over plums and leave to cool. Chill and serve with whipped cream and thin, crispy biscuits (cookies).

Rosy Apples

A very pretty autumn dish in which whole poached apples are filled with dried fruits. This recipe came about because in my restaurants in the autumn people often asked for baked apples — not a very easy last-minute pudding to do as our ovens were usually still busy roasting the season's game — so I devised this dish as a baked apple substitute.

30 fl oz (940 ml) water
8 oz (250 g) sugar
thinly pared peel of one orange
a few drops of red food colouring
6 eating apples
1 tablespoon mixed citrus (candied) peel
1 tablespoon currants
1 tablespoon chopped glacé cherries
1 tablespoon white wine
1 tablespoon white rum

In a large saucepan cook water, sugar and orange peel together over a gentle heat for 10 minutes. Remove from heat and add food colouring — test strength by dipping in a small piece of clean cloth and seeing if it takes the colour; the aim is to have rosy pink apples. Peel and core apples and poach very gently in syrup until tender but not broken. Remove from syrup and leave to cool. In a small pan place dried fruits, wine and rum, plus 1 tablespoon of the syrup, heat gently, stirring fruit, for 5 minutes. Leave to cool. To assemble arrange apples on a pretty serving dish, fill with fruit stuffing and pour round syrup. The stuffing is the only decoration needed.

Mocha Walnut Squares

This is a four-stage recipe but one well worth making. It is a classic from the walnut growing areas of France. I am indebted to Helge Rubinstein's Chocolate Book *for my own introduction to it. I have slightly changed the pastry base recipe. Like the chocolate cake, this improves with keeping on the larder shelf. It is delicious with coffee after a fresh fruit dessert, or makes a lovely present.*

PASTRY

2 oz (60g) butter

2 oz (60g) sugar

4 oz (125g) plain (all-purpose) flour, sieved

FILLING

2 oz (60g) butter

3 eggs

6 oz (185g) sugar

2 tablespoons strong black coffee

4 oz (125g) walnuts, roughly chopped

3 oz (90g) flour

COFFEE BUTTER ICING

2 oz (60g) unsalted butter

6 oz (185g) icing (powdered) sugar

2 tablespoons strong black coffee

CHOCOLATE ICING

5 oz (155g) plain (dark) chocolate

1 tablespoon dark rum

1½ oz (45g) butter

To make the pastry melt butter very slowly in a saucepan, do not allow to get too hot. Stir in sugar, leave to cool slightly, then add flour. Mix well together and press firmly into a 12 x 8 in (30 x 20 cm) Swiss roll (jelly roll) tin. Cook in a moderately hot oven, 200°C (400°F/ Gas 6) for 15 minutes. This pastry will not rise in the pan. Remove from oven and leave to cool.

To make the filling, gently soften butter in a small saucepan over a very low heat; it should not be runny for this recipe. Allow to cool before using. In a bowl beat together eggs and sugar until thick and fluffy. Slowly add coffee and softened butter; while still beating add walnuts and fold in flour. Pour this mixture over pastry base, spread evenly and return to the oven, 200°C (400°F/ Gas 6), and cook for 25-30 minutes.

Leave to cool while making icing.

To make coffee butter icing, beat butter and sugar together in a bowl until creamy and slowly add coffee. Beat well, then spread over walnut mixture, leave in a cool place until firm.

To make chocolate icing, melt chocolate with rum in a bowl over hot water. Remove from the heat and beat in butter a little at a time. Spread quickly over the coffee butter icing and leave to set.

Cut into small squares and store in an airtight box.

Spiced Apple Cake

A moist cake, crunchy with walnuts and a change from the usual gingerbread cake eaten at firework parties.

4 oz (125g) butter
6 oz (185g) soft brown sugar
1 egg, beaten
3 medium cooking (tart) apples, peeled and grated
1 teaspoon grated orange peel
1 teaspoon cinnamon
½ teaspoon ground cloves
8 oz (250g) self-raising flour
4 oz (125g) chopped walnuts

Line a 2 lb (1kg) loaf tin with greaseproof paper. Cream butter and sugar together in a bowl until light and fluffy. Stir in beaten egg, grated apple, orange peel and spices, then fold in flour. Add walnuts, mix again and pour into prepared loaf tin. Place in the oven and bake at 180°C (350°F/Gas 4) for 35-45 minutes or until cake is firm to the touch and springs back when pressed in the middle. Remove from oven and turn out onto a wire rack. Leave for 15 minutes before removing greaseproof paper. Serve in slices.

Autumn Punch

Warms the guests on Autumn evenings and goes well with the Spiced Apple Cake (above).

20 fl oz (625 ml) apple juice
1 apple stuck with 6 cloves
1 orange, sliced
32 fl oz (1 litre) still cider
6 fl oz (185 ml) Calvados

In a saucepan heat together apple juice, apple and cloves and sliced orange. Simmer for 10 minutes. Add cider, reheat to nearly boiling point, then add Calvados and serve.

The
Winter Kitchen

THE WINTER kitchen is for me both exhilarating and comforting. Winter, just like the other seasons, brings a supply of new ingredients to cook with.

A hundred years ago our ancestors spent the winter days cooking beef pudding, dumpling stews, jam roly-poly or plum duff and other solid foods to fill the hungry gap with. Dried fruits, vegetables and spices, pickles and preserves were the only ingredients that were available to break the monotony of the stodgy, filling dishes.

Now our shops and markets are full of out-of-season, imported foods which lighten the cook's chores and make for a much healthier diet.

There are mange tout (snow/sugar) peas to accompany a casserole and fresh strawberries for a coulis to pour round a dish of baked apples. Imported fresh vegetables and fruits may be expensive at this time but by using them carefully it is possible to cheer up our winter meals.

Cabbage has a dull and soggy reputation but, finely shredded, quickly blanched, drained and tossed in a frying pan with cream and dill seeds, it becomes an elegant vegetable.

If autumn is the season of fruits, winter is the season of roots; serve them hot, tossed with orange juice and butter, or cold as a salad. Celeriac is a lovely vegetable, tasting of celery but sweeter.

Celery Soup with Apples & Raisins

Winter is certainly a time for soups, warm and comforting. This is a favourite celery soup.

1 head celery
1 oz (30g) butter
1 medium onion, finely chopped
4 eating apples
2 oz (60g) raisins
a good pinch of allspice
10 fl oz (315 ml) cider
10 fl oz (315 ml) white stock
6 fl oz (185 ml) milk
4-6 fl oz (125-185 ml) single (light) cream
salt and pepper, to taste

Trim celery, discarding tough parts, and chop very finely using the leaves

as well. Melt butter in a saucepan, add onion and celery and stir-fry over a low heat for 8-10 minutes, taking care not to burn. Peel, core and chop apples. Add to saucepan with raisins and allspice, stir, add cider and stock, then cover and cook for 20-30 minutes until vegetables are very tender. Stir in milk, cream, salt and pepper, reheat and serve. If you like a thick soup, mix one tablespoon of cornflour (cornstarch) with a little of the milk in a bowl. Pour it into the soup once vegetables are cooked. Bring to the boil, then add rest of milk and cream.

Mushroom Roulade

A roulade is always a glamorous dish, it has something to do with the myth that a roulade is difficult to make at home. In fact it is very easy indeed, for it is only a soufflé-type mixture baked in a shallow tin rather than in a soufflé dish.

Serves 8 as a starter or 4-5 as a luncheon or supper dish.

ROULADE

2 oz (60g) butter

12 oz (375g) mushrooms, wiped clean

2 teaspoons chopped fresh marjoram
　　or 1 teaspoon dried oregano

1 oz (30g) plain (all-purpose) flour

8 fl oz (250ml) milk

3 eggs, separated

salt and pepper, to taste

FILLING

8 oz (250g) curd cheese

4 oz (125g) cooked ham

4 oz (125g) mushrooms, chopped

2 teaspoons chopped fresh marjoram
　　or 1 teaspoon dried oregano

2 tablespoons port or sherry

Grease a 12 x 8 in (30 x 20cm) Swiss roll (jelly roll) tin and line with non-stick parchment.

To make the roulade, melt 1 oz (30g) of the butter in a saucepan, add mushrooms and stir-fry for 3-5 minutes, then add herbs, cover and cook over a low heat for 8 minutes or until tender. Purée in a blender or food processor and reserve.

Melt remaining 1 oz (30g) butter in a saucepan over a low heat, then stir in flour. Slowly add milk, stirring constantly over a low heat until smooth, then increase heat until sauce boils and thickens. Remove from heat. Add egg yolks one by one to sauce, beating well in between. Stir in mushroom and herb purée, mixing well, then add salt and pepper. Whip egg whites in a clean bowl until very stiff and carefully fold into mushroom mixture. Pour into prepared tin and bake in a moderately hot oven, 200°C (400°F/Gas 6), for 10-15 minutes, or until mixture just shrinks from sides of baking tin. Remove from oven and leave to rest in tin for 5 minutes. Line a cooling rack with a clean teatowel and turn out roulade onto it. When cool, but not cold, remove lining paper.

To make the filling, place curd cheese and all other ingredients with salt and pepper in a blender or food processor and quickly blend together.

To assemble, spread filling over mushroom sponge and very gently roll up, with the help of the tea towel if necessary. Place on a heatproof serving dish, cover tightly with foil and reheat in the oven, at 200°C (400°F/ Gas 6), for 7-10 minutes. Serve in slices as you would a Swiss (jelly) roll, accompanied by a tomato salad.

Green Herb Pie

This pie, with its fresh greens and herbs, brings a taste of spring to late winter. Good for lunch or supper, served with a fresh carrot salad.

If you use a commercially-made shortcrust pastry you will need 8oz (250g).

6 oz (185g) plain (all-purpose) flour
pinch of salt
3 oz (90g) butter or margarine, very cold
2-4 tablespoons of ice cold water
12 oz (375g) chicken livers
1 lb (500g) leeks
8 oz (250g) spinach
1 bunch watercress, chopped
6 spring onions (scallions), chopped
1 bunch parsley, chopped
2 smoked bacon rashers, diced
3 eggs and 1 yolk
6 fl oz (185 ml) double (heavy) cream
pinch mace
pepper, to taste
milk, for glazing

Sift flour with salt into a bowl. Cut butter or margarine into small squares, add to flour and rub it in with finger-tips until mixture looks like bread-crumbs. Alternatively process flour, salt and butter in a food processor. Add 2 tablespoons of cold water and press mixture together until it forms a firm ball, you may need 3 or even 4 table-spoons of water, but add it slowly, the mixture must not become sticky. Cover pastry in plastic wrap and leave in the fridge while you prepare the pie filling.

Wash chicken livers and remove any discoloured bits, dry on absorbent kitchen paper and set aside.

Trim leeks, wash carefully, getting as much sand and soil as possible from green leaves. Pat dry and slice into rings ¼ in (0·5cm) thick; when you reach the green tops discard coarse outer leaves but continue to slice inner leaves ~ you should be able to use all of the leek. Wash, shake and dry spinach, and shred. Place leeks, spinach, watercress, spring onions, parsley and bacon in a bowl. Chop chicken livers, add to vegetables and mix together.

Break eggs into a bowl, add egg yolk and mix together with a fork until smooth, then add cream, mace, salt and pepper.

Butter a 2½ pint (1·8 litre) pie dish, fill with vegetables and meat, then pour over egg mixture.

Remove pastry from fridge, place on a floured work surface, lightly press into shape, then roll out to fit your pie dish. Place over vegetable mixture and press down onto the rim of the dish "fluting" as you go. Trim with a knife. Make leaves out of the trimmings and decorate. Cut a hole in the top of the pie, brush with milk and bake in a moderately hot oven, 200°C (400°F/Gas 6), for 30-45 minutes, until set in centre and golden brown. Should the top brown too quickly, cover lightly with foil.

Scallops in White Wine

18 scallops
2 oz (60g) butter
6 spring onions (scallions), chopped
1 bay leaf
20 fl oz (625ml) white wine
6 fl oz (185ml) double (heavy) cream
salt and pepper, to taste
2 tablespoons chopped fresh parsley

Wash scallops and carefully remove and reserve corals.

In a saucepan melt butter, add spring onions, bay leaf and white wine and bring to the boil. Add white pieces of scallop and poach for 4-5 minutes until just tender, adding corals 2 minutes before end of cooking time. Remove from stock with a slotted spoon and keep warm. Strain stock into a saucepan and reserve spring onions. Bring stock to the boil and reduce by half. Stir in cream, spring onions, salt and pepper; then add scallops, whites and corals, and gently reheat. Stir in chopped parsley and serve at once.

If you like a thicker sauce, add a beurre manié of 1 tablespoon flour and 1 tablespoon butter to stock, before you add cream.

Pheasant with Celery & Celeriac

Hen pheasants are more tender than cocks; even so I pot roast them to keep them as moist and succulent as possible.

2 oz (60g) butter
2 hen pheasants
1 medium onion,
  chopped
4 rashers streaky
  bacon, chopped
1 head of celery,
  thinly sliced
10 fl oz (315 ml)
  white wine
½ head celeriac,
  peeled and chopped
6 fl oz (185 ml) white stock
4 fl oz (125 ml) port
6 fl oz (185 ml) double (heavy) cream
salt and pepper, to taste

Melt butter in a large casserole over a medium heat, add birds and brown all over in butter, remove and set aside. Add onions, bacon and celery to casserole, stir-fry for 5 minutes, then return pheasants to pan, pour on wine, cover with a tight-fitting lid and cook for 50 minutes, until tender.

Meanwhile place celeriac and stock in a saucepan, bring to the boil, cover and cook for 20-25 minutes until tender. Place in a blender or food processor, add any juice, the port and cream, process to a purée. Return to saucepan and reserve.

When pheasants are cooked, transfer from casserole to a hot serving dish and place vegetables round them. Skim any fat off juices and stir juices into celeriac purée, adding salt and pepper. Reheat and serve in a sauceboat to accompany pheasants.

Sweet Carrots

Here is a simple way of cooking carrots, the butter and wine draw out their natural sweetness.

2 oz (60g) butter
1½ lb (750g) carrots, scraped and cut into
  eighths lengthwise
6 fl oz (185 ml) white wine
freshly ground white pepper, to taste

Melt butter in a saucepan, add carrots and stir-fry for 3-4 minutes. Pour in white wine, cover and simmer for 15 minutes or until vegetable is just tender. Remove lid, increase heat and reduce juices by half; add freshly ground white pepper and serve.

Jerusalem Artichokes & Yogurt Mayonnaise

These make an unusual starter or a good accompaniment to cold turkey after Christmas Day. They can be prepared in advance. The artichokes are easier to scrape if you do so as soon as you can after lifting them from the ground.

1½ lb (750g) Jerusalem artichokes, well scraped
juice of 2 oranges
1 tablespoon wine vinegar
4 fl oz (125 ml) olive or vegetable oil
salt and pepper, to taste
7 fl oz (220 ml) home made mayonnaise
5 fl oz (155 ml) plain yogurt
1 tablespoon chopped fresh parsley, to garnish

In a saucepan boil artichokes in salted water for 15-20 minutes, until tender. Drain, cool slightly, then, using a stainless steel knife, slice while still warm. Mix together orange juice, vinegar and oil in a bowl, add salt and pepper, then pour over warm artichokes and toss gently, making sure all slices are coated with dressing. Mix mayonnaise with yogurt and place in a serving dish. Serve artichokes cold, sprinkled with parsley and accompanied by the yogurt mayonnaise.

Winter Fruits in Mulled Wine

This is a wonderful winter fruit salad; sweet, spicy and warming on cold nights. Make extra and keep it, if you can, in a sealed jar in the fridge or larder.

4 oz (125g) currants
4 oz (125g) raisins
8 oz (250g) dried figs
6 oz (185g) prunes
2 hard eating apples, peeled and chopped
2 hard pears, peeled and chopped

4 oz (125g) walnuts, roughly chopped
2 in (5 cm) cinnamon stick
6 allspice
½ in (1 cm) piece of fresh ginger, chopped or ¼ teaspoon dried ginger
30 fl oz (940 ml) red wine
2 tablespoons honey

Place all ingredients in a large saucepan. Cover with a tight-fitting lid and simmer over a very low heat for ¾-1 hour. Cool and bottle. Serve with Lacy Biscuits (Cookies), see page 88.

Rüebli Torte

A light and delicious Swiss speciality very different from the usual moist carrot cake. I like to serve this as a pudding accompanied by single (light) cream. In Switzerland it is usually dusted with icing (powdered) sugar and decorated with miniature carrots made of coloured marzipan.

5 eggs, separated
8 oz (250g) sugar
3 oz (90g) plain (all-purpose) flour, sifted
8 oz (250g) ground almonds – skins left on
8 oz (250g) carrots, finely grated
icing (powdered) sugar, for dusting

Line a 10 in (25 cm) flan tin with non-stick parchment. Beat egg yolks and sugar together in a large bowl until pale and creamy and sugar is dissolved. In another bowl add flour to almonds and mix gently. Add carrots to egg yolks and mix lightly together, then add almond and flour mixture slowly, folding in lightly. Lastly beat egg whites until very stiff and fold carefully into egg mixture. Pour into prepared tin and bake at 180°C (350°F/Gas 4) for 40-50 minutes, or until beginning to shrink from sides of tin. Leave to cool in tin for 10 minutes before turning out onto a wire rack to cool. When almost cold remove parchment paper. To serve, dust with icing sugar. This cake keeps well for four to five days.

Seville Orange Curd

A refreshing change from lemon curd and not as sweet as ordinary orange curd. This recipe is useful as, unlike most curd recipes, it uses whole eggs.

2 Seville oranges
4 oz (125g) butter, cut into small pieces
8 oz (250g) sugar
3 eggs

Grate orange rind and squeeze juice into a heatproof bowl to fit the top of a double saucepan, add butter and sugar. Place saucepan over a low heat and cook mixture until all sugar is dissolved, 10-15 minutes. Break eggs into a bowl and beat well, then pour into orange mixture and cook, stirring constantly, until mixture thickens. Pot and cover as for Dark Green Mint Jelly, see page 47.

Christmas and Other Feasts

A CENTURY AGO our year was broken up by numerous feasts and festivals, some deriving from pagan celebrations from our pre-Christian past. There were also many more country festivals and fairs, often with music and dancing, to celebrate events which seem to us now to have been very unlikely occasions for throwing a party: summer and winter solstices, the advent of spring, fairs for labour hiring, strawberry fairs and, amazing though it may seem, a celebration at the time of the paying of the half-yearly rents and tithes. Now we generally celebrate only Harvest, Christmas, New Year, Easter and a few national holidays, and family occasions such as weddings, christenings, birthdays and bar mitzvahs.

Although entertaining has become much less formal and the preparations simpler, our feasts do still include some traditional foods. Turkey for Thanksgiving or Christmas is the obvious example. Families themselves create their own traditions and pass them down over the years.

Feasts and celebrations need careful planning whether your party is for two or twenty. I have found that the most successful parties are those at which the hostess is relaxed because she knows her meal is either in casserole form or in some other state where it requires little last minute attention.

A favourite of our family, prepared in advance and now almost a Christmas tradition, is this delicious citrus fruit-based Festive Starter.

Festive Starter

Light, refreshing and most unusual.

Serves 10-12

2 grapefruit
4 oranges
1½ lb (750g) grapes, black or green
2 tablespoons chopped fresh parsley
4 spring onions (scallions), chopped
6 fl oz (185ml) vinaigrette (made with
⅔ olive oil, ⅓ wine vinegar)
freshly ground black pepper
sprig of parsley, to decorate

Peel and remove all pith and stringy bits from grapefruit and oranges, chop into bite-sized pieces; skin, halve and seed grapes. Place all fruit in a bowl, add parsley and spring onions, pour over vinaigrette, toss gently, cover and leave in a cool place for several hours or overnight. I think it better not left in the fridge. Just before serving add two or three twists of black pepper from a pepper mill. Serve in individual dishes, decorated with a sprig of parsley.

Spiced Cashew Nuts

To serve with drinks.

1 tablespoon cooking oil
1 teaspoon curry powder
6 oz (185 g) cashew nuts

Heat oil in a heavy saucepan over a low heat, add curry powder and stir well, then add cashew nuts and stir-fry over a low heat until nuts are well coated with oil and begin to turn golden brown. Remove from pan and drain on absorbent kitchen paper. Store in an airtight tin, eat within a week.

Carrot & Cucumber Cocktail Bites

These vegetable bites stay crisp, so they can be prepared in advance, laid out on a serving platter, covered with plastic wrap and left in a cool place or the fridge for several hours.

Choose medium-sized carrots, scrape, slice thinly and drop into a bowl of iced water. Wash a cucumber, halve lengthwise and remove seeds, sprinkle with a little salt and leave to drain upside down on absorbent kitchen paper for half an hour. In a bowl beat together 6 oz (185 g) curd cheese, 1 tablespoon yogurt and salt and pepper to taste. Divide the mixture into two and to one half add 2 teaspoons grated horseradish and to the other half 1 tablespoon finely chopped gherkin (dill pickle). Remove carrots from water and pat dry on a clean teatowel, spread with horseradish mixture and decorate with a pinch of paprika. Wipe cucumber dry, slice into ¾ in (2 cm) pieces and fill centres with gherkin (dill pickle) mixture, decorate with a tiny sprig of parsley.

Smoked Salmon Quiche

A real party quiche with rich, crumbly pastry and wonderful smoked salmon filling. I like to make this in a tart tin with a removable base. Use a 10 in (25cm) tart tin.

PASTRY
6 oz (185g) plain (all-purpose) flour
pinch of salt
4 oz (125g) butter
2-3 tablespoons ice cold water

PIE FILLING
6 oz (185g) curd cheese
3 whole eggs and 1 yolk
6 fl oz (185ml) single (light) cream
pinch mace
salt and pepper, to taste
12 oz (375g) smoked salmon

TO GARNISH
slices of cucumber
thin slices of lemon

Sift flour with salt into a mixing bowl. Rub fat into flour until it looks like fine breadcrumbs, then add water, a tablespoon at a time – you may not need it all. Press dough together until it forms a firm ball, wrap in greaseproof paper and leave in a cold place for ½-1 hour. Meanwhile prepare the filling.

In a blender or food processor, combine curd cheese, eggs, egg yolk, cream, mace, salt and pepper. Blend thoroughly. Fold in smoked salmon and set aside.

Remove pastry from fridge, place on a floured board and roll out slightly larger than the tart tin. Fit into tin, trim edges, cover with a circle of greaseproof paper, sprinkle with dried peas or beans and bake blind at 190°C (375°F/ Gas 5) for 15 minutes. Remove from oven, take out beans and paper and pour smoked salmon mixture into quiche base. Reduce oven temperature and bake at 180°C (350°F/Gas 4) for 30-45 minutes, or until set in centre. Serve warm or cold, decorated with slices of cucumber and thin slices of lemon. A green salad is a good accompaniment.

Pastry tip: I find it much easier to press the pastry mixture into the tin rather than roll it out. When you add the water to the flour and fat, use a knife to combine it and don't press the mixture into a ball, leave it in the crumb stage. Cover the bowl and leave in a cool place to rest. To make the case, press the pastry crumb mixture out onto the bottom of the tin and press up the sides. This makes a very light pastry.

Seafood Ragoût

This is a lovely festive dish for a buffet party — summer or winter. It is very easy to prepare and can be got ready in advance and put together fifteen to twenty minutes before serving. Serves 8-10 lavishly.

4 oz (125g) butter
8 spring onions (scallions), chopped
2 teaspoons paprika
1 tablespoon tomato purée
2 lb (1 kg) cooked prawns
2 lb (1 kg) cooked chicken, diced
8 fl oz (250 ml) dry sherry
12 fl oz (375 ml) double (heavy) cream
6 fl oz (185 ml) plain yogurt
salt and pepper, to taste
sprigs of parsley to decorate and, if
    possible, a few prawns in their shells

If you like to assemble this dish at the last minute have everything prepared, weighed and measured out.

In a large chafing dish melt butter, add spring onions, paprika and tomato purée and stir-fry for 1-2 minutes over a low heat, then add prawns and stir-fry for a further 1-2 minutes. Add cooked chicken and sherry, stir-fry for 3-4 minutes or until the chicken is hot through. Stir in cream, yogurt, salt and pepper and reheat, but do not boil. Serve either in a chafing dish or on a large, heated serving dish. Decorate with sprigs of parsley and prawns. Serve with plain boiled rice.

Stuffed Duck Breasts for Two

This is a favourite dinner party dish. It is luxurious and unusual but easy to prepare in advance and the last minute cooking time is short. This dish can also be served cold as a starter; slice the duck breasts thinly and serve with Kumquats in White Wine (see page 50) and sprigs of watercress. As a starter two duck breasts serve four people.

1 pair duck breasts, skinned and
    trimmed of all fat
2 oz (60g) butter
1 teaspoon finely chopped onion
2 oz (60g) chicken livers
1 tablespoon brandy
salt and pepper, to taste
1 teaspoon grated orange peel
1 oz (30g) walnuts, chopped
2 tablespoons port
juice of 1 orange
1 teaspoon redcurrant jelly

Using a sharp knife make an incision in each duck breast near top of breast. Push knife through this until blade comes out at the opposite end, making a hollow right through the length of the breast, into which you can push the stuffing. Make this hollow as wide as possible without actually splitting the flesh.

Melt 1 oz (30g) of the butter in a frying pan, add onion and cook gently for 5-6 minutes. Add chicken livers and cook for a further 5 minutes, turning half way through cooking.

Remove pan from heat. Using a fork mash or crush chicken livers to a paste, add brandy, salt and pepper, orange peel and walnuts. Mix well and stuff duck breasts with this mixture.

In the same frying pan melt remaining butter, heat gently, add stuffed duck breasts and cook over a medium heat for 5-6 minutes on each side. Remove to a serving dish and keep warm. Pour port and orange juice into frying pan, add redcurrant jelly, salt and pepper and bring to the boil. Boil for one minute, then pour round the duck breasts. Decorate with kumquats in white wine, if desired, and serve with a watercress and orange salad and puréed potatoes.

Sally's Four Birds

This is a party recipe. I adapted it in my restaurant mainly to use up such things as duck legs ~ left over after using the breasts for stuffing and serving on their own ~ guinea fowl legs and pigeon legs were also often left over from other dishes. The birds you use can be of your own choice. It is a delicious dish and worth making from scratch. I give the recipe without using left-overs, but you can adapt it to suit the ingredients available. It serves 14-16.

1 pheasant
2 pigeons
1 duck
1 small chicken
3 tangerines
4 oz (125 g) butter
1 medium onion, chopped
4 oz (125 g) streaky bacon, chopped
1 carrot, peeled and grated
1 lb (500 g) prunes, stoned
pinch ground allspice
juice of 3 oranges
8 fl oz (250 ml) port
10 fl oz (315 ml) single (light) cream
6 fl oz (185 ml) plain yogurt
salt and pepper, to taste
2 tablespoons chopped fresh parsley, to finish

Remove breasts from all the birds and reserve, cut off legs and wings, remove oysters. Skin and trim fat off legs and joint. Remove peel from tangerines and reserve. Melt 2 oz (60 g) of the butter in a large casserole, add onion and fry gently for 5 minutes. Add legs, wings and other pieces of the birds, together with bacon, carrot, prunes, tangerine peel, allspice, orange juice and port. Bring to the boil, cover with a tight-fitting lid and simmer for 30-45 minutes, or until meat is tender but not dry. Melt remaining 2 oz (60 g) of butter in a frying pan and fry breasts, they will vary in the length of cooking, the duck breasts taking the longest. Fry them in relays, starting with the pigeons ~ 2-3 minutes each side, chicken ~ 2-3 minutes each side, pheasant ~ 3-4 minutes each side, duck ~ 5-7 minutes each side. You will need to cook the meats a little longer if you like them well done. Remove from pan and keep warm. If you like cut the larger pieces of meat to the size of the pigeon breasts.

Remove tangerine peel from casserole and add cream, yogurt, salt and pepper, together with the breasts. Reheat but do not boil. Leave to rest for 5-6 minutes. Add the tangerines, quartered and pips removed. Sprinkle with parsley and serve.

I like to accompany this with baked potatoes and a celery, apple and walnut salad.

To Roast a Turkey and Keep it Succulent

Stuff your bird in the normal way, then, instead of covering the bird with buttered paper, make a paste of flour and water ~ it should look and feel like pastry. Press out to the size you need to cover your bird leaving only its legs and wings uncovered. Cook in the normal way but allow one to two minutes extra cooking time per 1 lb (500g). You will find that the legs of the bird are cooked and the breast moist and full of flavour. If you do not wish to stuff the bird, fill the cavity tightly with a peeled onion, apples and an orange. Remove crust 10-15 minutes before end of cooking time and return to oven to brown. This is a good way to roast game birds which tend to be dry.

Christmas Turkey Hash

This doesn't sound festive but it tastes quite delicious, is quick to prepare and is an excellent way of using up cold turkey to make a lovely after-Christmas lunch dish. Serves 8-10.

4 oz (125 g) butter
1 medium onion, chopped
3 cooking (tart) apples, peeled, cored and chopped
3 eating apples, peeled, cored and chopped
2 sprigs rosemary
10 fl oz (315 ml) white wine
2-3 lb (1-1.5 kg) cold cooked turkey, trimmed, cut into 1 in (2.5 cm) cubes
6 fl oz (185 ml) single (light) cream
6 fl oz (185 ml) plain yogurt
salt and pepper, to taste

Melt butter in a saucepan over a low heat, add onion and cook for 5-6 minutes, then add apples, rosemary and 2 tablespoons of the white wine. Cover and leave to cook for 20-25 minutes over a low heat. Remove rosemary sprigs, add turkey and rest of white wine, bring to the boil and heat through. Stir in cream, yogurt, salt and pepper, and reheat gently but do not boil. This is good served with a dish of curry-flavoured rice to which you have added three or four chopped spring onions (scallions) and some chopped toasted almonds.

Three Party Salads

BAKED APPLE SALAD

For each person allow 1 small eating apple. Core in the usual way, stuff the centre of the apples with chopped onion and rosemary, place on a baking tray, pour over some cider—for four apples you would need 5 fl oz (155 ml) cider—and bake at 180°C (350°F/Gas 4) for 30-40 minutes until tender. When apples are cooked and cold remove onions and rosemary and fill the hollows with your favourite potato salad mixture. Arrange prettily on a serving dish and decorate with sprigs of parsley and slices of cucumber. This salad is particularly good with a fish dish.

OLIVE & GRAPE SALAD

A very pretty salad, quick and simple.

1 cup green grapes, seeded and halved
1 cup black olives, stoned
1 teaspoon chopped onion
1 tablespoon chopped mixed herbs
4 fl oz (125 ml) Orange Vinaigrette, see
    below
freshly ground black pepper

Mix all ingredients together in a bowl and leave to marinate for 3-4 hours. Like the Festive Starter, this dish is better not refrigerated.

GREEN BEAN SALAD

1 red pepper (capsicum), skinned and
    chopped
1 lb (500 g) cooked cold green beans
½ medium onion, finely chopped
1 tablespoon tomato purée
¼ teaspoon chilli pepper
1 clove garlic, crushed
1 teaspoon honey or sugar
4 fl oz (125 ml) vinaigrette
salt, to taste

To skin the pepper, hold it on a fork or skewer over a naked flame, keep turning it until it is blackened all over, then drop it into a bowl of cold water and rub skin off. Remove from water, dry on absorbent kitchen paper, cut away seeds and chop into small pieces.

Place beans, pepper and onion in a bowl and mix well together. In another bowl mix tomato purée, chilli, garlic, honey or sugar, vinaigrette and salt. Pour over beans and leave for 30 minutes before serving.

Orange Vinaigrette

2 teaspoons grated orange peel
2 teaspoons vinegar
4 tablespoons orange juice

8 tablespoons olive oil
½ teaspoon Dijon mustard
salt and pepper, to taste

In a screw-top jar mix all ingredients together and shake well. Store in a cool place and use as needed.

Black Forest Trifle

This makes a scrumptious dessert and looks very festive. Start at least a day in advance. Serves 10-12.

CHOCOLATE SPONGE

4 oz (125g) butter
4 oz (125g) sugar
2 eggs, beaten
4 oz (125g) self-raising flour
1 oz (30g) cocoa powder
1-2 tablespoons milk

FOR TRIFLE

4 tablespoons brandy, or other suitable liqueur
16 oz (500g) jar black Morello cherries, drained, juice reserved
12 macaroons, coarsely crushed
20 fl oz (625ml) homemade custard prepared to your favourite recipe
10 fl oz (315ml) double (heavy) cream
6 fl oz (185ml) single (light) cream
10 fl oz (315ml) Chocolate Sauce, see below
4 oz (125g) plain (dark) chocolate, grated

Line two 9in (22.5cm) sponge tins with greaseproof paper. Cream butter and sugar together in a bowl until pale and creamy. Beat in eggs gradually, mixing well. Sift flour with cocoa powder and fold into egg mixture. Stir in a little milk to mix to a dropping consistency. Pour mixture into prepared tins and bake at 190°C (375°F/Gas 5) for 10-15 minutes until firm to the touch. Turn out onto wire racks and leave until cold.

Split chocolate sponges in half and sprinkle with brandy. Line a pretty glass bowl with a layer of chocolate cake, sprinkle again with some of the cherry juice if you like a moist trifle.

Cover cake with a layer of cherries, sprinkle over some of the macaroons, then pour over some of the custard. Mix two creams together and whip until stiff, then spread a thin layer of cream over custard. Pour over a little chocolate sauce. Repeat until you have used up all the ingredients, finishing with a layer of cream and a drizzle of chocolate sauce. Sprinkle liberally with grated chocolate. Chill before serving.

CHOCOLATE SAUCE

8 oz (250g) plain (dark) chocolate, broken into squares
6 fl oz (185ml) single (light) cream
1 oz (30g) butter
2 teaspoons golden (corn) syrup
2 teaspoons orange liqueur

Place all ingredients in a saucepan and melt slowly over a low heat. Cool before serving.

Cousin Sonny's Plum Pudding

This recipe is very light, is packed with fruit and contains no suet. The quantities given make two 1½ pint (940ml) bowls and one 1 pint (625ml). I make the full recipe and keep those we don't need. I have kept them for a full two years stored on a cool shelf in the larder; but if you are worried about keeping the puddings this way, keep them in the freezer.

10 oz (315g) raisins
10 oz (315g) sultanas (golden raisins)
6 oz (185g) currants
6 oz (185g) glacé cherries, cut in quarters
6 oz (185g) prunes, stoned and chopped
4 oz (125g) blanched almonds, roughly chopped
8 oz (250g) butter
6 oz (185g) dark brown sugar
4 eggs
8 oz (250g) finely grated carrot
grated peel of one lemon
8 oz (250g) breadcrumbs
2 oz (60g) plain (all-purpose) flour
½ teaspoon mace
1 teaspoon cinnamon
1 teaspoon garam masala
4 fl oz (125ml) brandy

Mix all fruit and nuts together in a large bowl.

In another large bowl cream butter and sugar together until pale and creamy, add eggs, one by one, beating well in between; then add carrot, lemon peel and breadcrumbs. Sift flour with spices and stir into egg mixture. Now add fruits and nuts a handful at a time, mixing well and, lastly, fold in brandy. Fill the pudding basins as described below and boil in the top of a double boiler for 6 hours. Re-boil for a further 2 hours before eating.

Lining a pudding basin: I find the simplest way to line a pudding basin is to line it with foil first. Cut off a piece of foil, leaving enough to fold over and cover the pudding once it is in the bowl. Place foil round the outside of the bowl and shape it carefully, taking care not to puncture it; now place it inside the bowl, press to fit. Next line inside of foil with buttered greaseproof paper, leaving enough to fold over the top and cover, or cut a circle to fit. Fill the bowls, wrap over greaseproof paper and foil. You now have a watertight protection for your puddings and they turn out perfectly. Should you wish to keep the puddings for a year or two leave until quite cold and firm, then carefully peel off foil and greaseproof paper and wrap in clean wrappings. The puddings are best stored for 4-6 weeks before eating.

Christmas Tart

Use the Nectarine Tart recipe for this, see page 87, and add to the egg and cream mixture four tablespoons of your favourite mincemeat, one tablespoon chopped cherries and one tablespoon chopped almonds. Cook in the usual way. Serve with Rum Sauce.

Rum Sauce

Much nicer than Hard Sauce and now a family tradition with us.

1 cup double (heavy) cream
4 eggs
½ cup icing (powdered) sugar
¼ cup dark rum

Whip cream in a bowl until thick. Over a saucepan of hot water whip eggs and icing sugar in another bowl until very stiff and creamy, then leave to cool. Fold rum into cream, then fold in egg mixture, pour into a pretty bowl and ladle onto puddings and tarts.

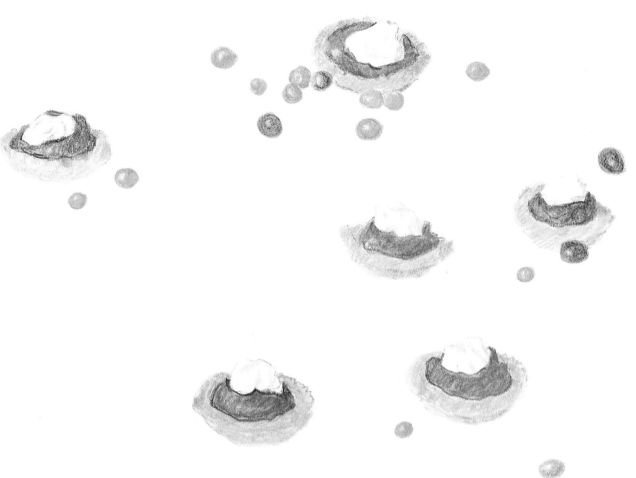

Spiced Cranberry Toasts

Unusual and very pretty, use with summer fruits or apple purée in the autumn.
The spiced toast could just as well be called 'Lazy Cook's Pastry'.

2 cups cranberries
2 whole tangerines, skins included
12 oz (375g) sugar
4 tablespoons white rum

FOR THE TOAST
2-3 oz (60-90g) butter
6 slices white bread
2 oz (60g) caster (superfine) sugar
2 teaspoons ground cinnamon
whipped cream, to decorate

Place fruit, sugar and rum in a blender or food processor and process until smooth but not completely puréed.

Butter liberally some slices of white bread, dust with a mixture of caster sugar and cinnamon, cut into circles and press into well greased patty tins. Bake at 190°C (375°F/Gas 5), for 4-6 minutes or until golden and crisp. Remove from oven and leave to cool. Fill with cranberry mixture, top with whipped cream.

White Fruit Cake

This is an extravagant cake, but well worth it. Use the very best fruits you can afford.

4 oz (125g) walnuts, skinned and chopped
8 oz (250g) crystallised pineapple
6 oz (185g) glacé cherries
6 oz (185g) dried peach halves
6 oz (185g) dried pear halves
6 oz (185g) dried apricot halves
4 oz (125g) chopped mixed citrus
        (candied) peel
2 oz (60g) angelica
8 oz (250g) butter
6 oz (185g) white sugar
4 eggs
grated peel of 1 lemon
8 oz (250g) ground almonds
4-6 tablespoons milk
10 oz (315g) self-raising flour
4 tablespoons white rum, to pour over
        after cooking

To skin walnuts, place in a saucepan, cover with milk, bring to the boil and leave to simmer for 3-4 minutes. Leave until cool enough to handle — the skins will peel off quite easily and the walnuts taste much sweeter and rather like fresh walnuts. Discard the milk.

Line a 9 in (22·5 cm) round cake tin, 3½ in (8 cm) deep, with foil and greaseproof paper as described in Cousin Sonny's Plum Pudding, see page 127. Mix all the fruit and the walnuts together in a large bowl. In another large bowl cream butter and sugar together, add the eggs one by one, beating well in between, then stir in lemon peel. Beat in ground almonds, stir in 4 tablespoons of the milk and fold in flour. If the mixture seems very stiff, add 1 or 2 more tablespoons of milk. Fold in fruit and nuts carefully. Pour into prepared cake tin and bake at 150°C (300°F/Gas 2) for 4-5 hours. This is a large cake and needs long, slow cooking. Leave to cool in tin, then turn out onto a wire rack, prick base and pour over rum. Rewrap in greaseproof paper then foil to store.

I don't ice this cake, but decorate it either with glacé fruits for a special party cake or marzipan fruits for Christmas.

Salt Dough

This is a recipe for making traditional Central European Christmas decorations. They are inedible. Once baked, the designs can be painted, but I think they look prettiest left their natural colour. A closed order of nuns in Switzerland makes exquisite angels out of this dough, where they are a traditional Christmas tree decoration.

4 cups flour
1 cup salt
½ cup water

Mix ingredients together in a bowl, they should have the consistency of bread dough. Knead well, trying not to get any air pockets in the mixture as these spoil the decorations and cause breakages. Divide dough into three and roll out to ¼ in (0·5 cm) thick, cut into shapes, such as stars, angels, fish, sheep, bells or wreaths. The wreath-shape can be achieved very simply by cutting out a circle of dough with a large cutter and a hole in the centre with a smaller cutter.

At this stage you can decorate the shapes by inscribing, with a sharpish knitting needle or a not-too-sharp pencil, the folds of the angel's robe or the squiggles of the sheep's wool. Or, instead of inscribing decoration, you can apply it. To a wreath, for example, you can apply leaves and flowers cut out from the dough and pressed on with a little water. At this point don't forget to make holes at the top of your shapes, about the size of a knitting needle (they will shrink during baking). Now lay on ungreased baking sheets and bake in a very slow oven at 120°C (250°F/Gas ½) for 4-5 hours, or until pale and crisp. Cool on wire cooling racks and when cold glaze with a clear household varnish. They keep from one year to the next, but like glass balls they are fragile and, like biscuits, need to be kept in an airtight container. Thread shapes with gold or silver string to hang on your Christmas tree.

Pot Pourri

This makes a lovely present. It is easy to make yourself, much nicer than any bought pot pourri, and it's fun to do. Not all the flowers for this pot pourri will be out at the same time, but the idea is to gather, dry and store them, then make your own mixture.

You will need: 6 handfuls of mixed sweet-smelling petals: lilacs, roses, pinks, stocks, jasmin, sweet peas, nicotiana, mignonette; any sweet-smelling petals from your garden — or other people's.

Spread the petals out on trays and dry in the sun indoors; even in the finest weather there is too much moisture in the air for reliable drying outside. When your petals are completely dry, store lightly packed in polythene bags and seal. When you have the required amount, place in a large bowl and add 1 lb (500g) fine sea salt, 1 oz (30g) crushed cloves, 2 oz (60g) crushed allspice, the grated peel of 1 lemon, 1 grated nutmeg, thinly pared peel of 2 oranges and 1 oz (30g) powdered orris root ~ obtainable from a chemist shop (drug store). Mix well and add a handful of rosemary and thyme and a small handful each of mint and marjoram.

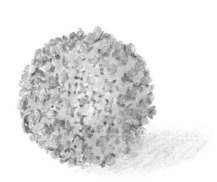

Pomander Balls

Pomanders are lovely, but to stick a large orange full of cloves can be a tedious and nail-breaking task; so try limes — they make very fragrant pomanders — or kumquats.

To make: choose perfect fruits and good long cloves. Insert the cloves evenly all over the fruit, their heads just touching. Tie with a fine ribbon and hang to dry. The scent can be intensified by rolling the pomander in a mixture of spice and orris root, but I have kept pomanders in my drawers for some time and they keep their tangy scent of cloves and orange. The smell goes musty and dusty if hung for any length of time in a warm room.

The Wine Rack

EATING STYLES have changed: what we eat now is very different from what we were eating ten or fifteen years ago. Wine drinking, I feel, has also changed, though perhaps more recently.

Our own drinking tastes have changed not only because the cost of the classic fine wines puts them out of reach for family kitchen suppers, but also because the range and quality of wines available have improved vastly since the days when 'Spanish' was used only for cooking and even then there was a chance that it might turn a white fish grey during its poaching.

I don't think I could put it better than my friend Robin Woodhouse when he says: "Twenty years ago, the classic progression for a formal dinner in England ran something like this: Champagne as apéritif, white Burgundy with Dover Sole, Claret with lamb, Sauternes with the dessert, then Vintage Port to round off the meal.

"The serious wine lover (with a pocket to match) will still plan a similar wine list for special gatherings. Other wine lovers (including most wine merchants!) unable to afford such luxury, will try to work in the occasional classic wine which comes their way. Great examples of these wines are still unmatched in terms of style, complexity and subtlety but they have to be very carefully chosen and the price is extremely high.

"Fortunately, however, we live in the Golden Age for wine lovers. There is now more good wine available, at all price levels, than ever before for our delight. This is mainly due to increased winemaking knowledge and skill. The impetus came, to a large extent, from winemakers in the U.S.A. and Australia with their keenness and freedom to experiment; their example is already having a radical effect on the wine scene in Europe.

"In essence, these 'new wave' wines combine maximum freshness and cleanness with 'fruit' and varietal character. Although the aim, in many cases, is directly to emulate the classics, good wine always reflects its origins, so that exciting new styles are being born rather than look-alikes stealing the limelight.

"The recipes in this book mirror a similar movement away from a limited range of classic dishes towards a freer approach to ingredients, combinations and traditions. I offer a few suggestions for wines to accompany some of them. I have purposely avoided the well-known and expensive names.

"With the Avocado Soup (opposite page) I suggest an off-dry Muscat from Portugal or Alsace for the wonderful aroma of fresh grapes.

"For the Fish Pie with Lemon Balm (page 72) I should like to serve one of the new Sauvignon Blancs from New Zealand with their pure 'gooseberry' fruit.

"One can happily drink anything with chicken, but with the Yogurt Poussin (page 73) a Chardonnay from Australia or California for rich oaky taste is a good choice.

"Claret is made for lamb. Here are three inexpensive substitutes: Portuguese Garrafeira, Cabernet from northern Italy and Californian Merlot.

"The Rabbit with Bacon & Prunes (page 24) immediately brings to mind both Hunter River Shiraz from Australia and top-level Spanish red.

"The delicacy of flavour in vegetarian dishes is, I think, best matched by red and white wine from the Loire Valley. A good Sauvignon

de Touraine, with its aromatic bouquet and crisp acidity, would partner Flageolet Beans with Dill (page 18) very well.

"Desserts are always difficult. The old classic – Sauternes – is to my mind better on its own; it can even take the place of dessert! The wines that I find most useful are sweet Muscats of all sorts and Madeira – this goes a long way and the opened bottle will keep for ages too.

"Finally, two suggestions for informal and party use: Colombard, from California or the southwest of France is an excellent soft, fresh white which is off-dry – good on its own or with light food and Bulgarian Cabernet is really unbeatable as a cheap red with considerable style."

Avocado Soup

Avocado soup is often served slightly spiced, but try this soup flavoured with sherry. This recipe serves four.

3 avocados
1 teaspoon grated orange peel
2 teaspoons chopped fresh marjoram
30 fl oz (940 ml) white stock
6 fl oz (185 ml) dry sherry
salt and pepper, to taste
½ tablespoon sesame seeds, to finish

Peel, halve and remove stones from avocados. Place in a blender or food processor and purée, then add orange peel, marjoram and 10 fl oz (315 ml) of stock. Process again briefly to mix. Heat remaining stock in a saucepan to boiling point. Stir in purée, sherry, salt and pepper and reheat gently – do not boil. Serve hot or cold, sprinkled with sesame seeds.

The Wine Rack

Trout Poached in White Wine

This recipe is particularly good for farmed trout whose flavour is perhaps not quite as good as that of wild trout. It uses wine only for the poaching but is not as wasteful as you might think, for the cooking liquor can be kept, frozen and used for fish stock.

4 medium to large trout, heads removed
    and cleaned
2 oz (60g) butter
10 fl oz (315 ml) dry white wine
salt and pepper, to taste
2 tablespoons chopped fresh dill
4 tablespoons double (heavy) cream

Wash trout inside and out, dry with absorbent kitchen paper. Melt butter in a large frying pan, add trout and cook gently for 2 minutes on each side, then pour over wine and add salt and pepper. Poach over a low heat for 4 minutes on each side, or until just cooked; then, using a slotted spoon, transfer to a heated platter and keep warm. Pour off half the cooking liquor, add dill and bring to a fast boil. Boil for 2 minutes, add cream, pour over fish and serve at once. Plain boiled potatoes and a hot cucumber dish are good with this.

Sole with Vermouth & Green Peppercorns

In my restaurants I often served sole cooked this way.

For each fish, weighing ¾ - 1lb (375-500g), you will need:

1 oz (30g) butter
½ teaspoon green peppercorns
4 tablespoons sweet white vermouth
1 teaspoon chopped fresh chives
2 teaspoons chopped fresh parsley

Have the fishmonger clean, skin and remove heads from sole, but leave

it on the bone. Wash fish inside and out, making sure it is thoroughly clean inside. Dry well on absorbent kitchen paper. Melt butter in a large frying pan, add sole and cook very gently for 5-6 minutes on each side; the secret of this dish is to cook the sole so gently that you scarcely think it could be cooking. After 2 minutes on the second side, add peppercorns and vermouth, basting fish well. To serve, place on a heated platter, pour over pan juices and sprinkle with herbs.

Chicken Breasts with Yogurt & Fresh Herbs

This was another popular restaurant dish.

For two people you will need:

1 teaspoon butter
2 medium to large chicken breasts
2 teaspoons chopped fresh basil
1 teaspoon chopped fresh chives
1 tablespoon medium sherry
1 tablespoon double (heavy) cream
salt and pepper, to taste
1 tablespoon thick plain yogurt

Heat butter in a frying pan, but do not allow to brown. Add chicken breasts and fry very gently for 3-4 minutes on each side. After 2 minutes' cooking on the second side, add herbs and sherry. Transfer chicken breasts to a hot platter and keep warm. Add cream to pan juices and bring to the boil. Boil for 1 minute, stir in salt, pepper and yogurt, then pour over chicken breasts and serve at once. I serve this dish with a small selection of crudités, which are delicious dipped in the sauce.

Vegetables

Vegetables are often improved by a tablespoon or two of one of the fortified wines. To cooked spinach add two to three tablespoons Marsala, with a knob of butter, it makes a superb dish. Try a little medium dry sherry with celery or mashed potatoes.

Carrots are good sweated in white wine and butter; mushrooms are wonderful cooked in butter and sherry and served with a little cream mixed in; end-of-season beans are also enhanced by sherry. Keep experimenting.

Cook's Nips

Ideally, a cool glass of Chassagne Montrachet: more likely a glass of Bulgarian Chardonnay, laced with sparkling mineral water.

Index